YOR

General E
of Stirling
University

Joseph Conrad

NOSTROMO

Notes by Anthony Strange

LONGMAN
YORK PRESS

YORK PRESS
Immeuble Esseily, Place Riad Solh, Beirut.

LONGMAN GROUP LIMITED
London
Associated companies, branches and representatives throughout the world

First published 1980
ISBN 0 582 78223 6
Printed in Hong Kong by
Wing Tai Cheung Printing Co Ltd

Contents

Part 1

Introduction

JOSEPH CONRAD'S LIFE—the early part at least—was an exceptional one for an English writer. Born in Poland in 1857—his real name was Josef Konrad Korzeniowski—he did not come under English influence or begin to learn the English language till he was over twenty. Even then it was not a question of living in the country of his adoption, but, for many years, only of sailing round the world in British ships, coming into contact with British sailors together with all the innumerable other types of men, of all colours and races, that constant travels offer for observation.

Conrad's childhood in Poland may have left him some happy memories, but circumstances and the historical period in which he was born decided that his home life should be broken up early. His mother died before he was in his teens, and his father too. But there was a further tragedy behind this, for his father's death was largely brought on by the cares and hardship of exile in Siberia, where he was sent in punishment by the then Russian masters of the part of Poland in which he lived, for he had idealistically but injudiciously taken part in a revolution that had failed. At that time Poland was still divided into three, under Russia, Prussia and Austria, whose combined might kept the country tightly under control in spite of the Poles' ill-organised attempts to gain independence. Conrad's family had a mainly aristocratic background, and his childhood experiences left the boy with the burning patriotism felt by so many Poles; in after years, to describe the situation of his youth, Conrad used the phrase: 'the oppressive shadow of the great Russian Empire'. Another result of his youthful experiences was that there always remained present in his mind the twin ideas of duty and leadership. Men like his father showed others how to live and, though Conrad described his father as a man 'of exalted and dreamy temperament', meaning that he was too much of an idealist to be practical, Conrad never lost his boyhood power of admiration. Conrad always respected a man with a strong sense of duty and courage enough to follow it. When he met other such men in life, he treasured their memory and he drew their portraits again and again in his stories.

Conrad described how, when he was young, he spent long hours studying the maps of distant countries and then he would put his finger on the large open spaces and say: 'When I grow up, I shall go there.' This was the beginning of his passion for travel and for exploration both by land and sea. With such a temperament, it was not likely that he would remain for long at home. After his parents' deaths, he was under the care of his mother's brother and once he had begun to feel this deep need to travel, Conrad never ceased worrying his uncle to give him permission to go abroad. Finally, at seventeen, he was provided with money and he made his way to France, for French was the only foreign language he knew at that time, and the following year he embarked on a French ship on his first voyage. However, there was clearly something which attracted him to England and the English, and when he joined his first British ship two years later in 1878, he began to learn the language. He was always an adventurous man, as can be seen, but here began another type of adventure, which proved to be equally important for him, that is to say, adventure with words. We shall see later when we look closely at his writing how full it is of a sense of enjoyment derived from the use of the English language which he began so late and in which, when speaking, he always retained a foreign accent. Right to the end of his life it was obvious from everything he wrote what pleasure he got from handling the words and phrases of the language that he found so expressive; we notice the way in which he brings them out and, as it were, rolls them round his tongue. He himself said about the English language: 'its very idioms had a direct action on my temperament and fashioned my still plastic character'. The result is a freshness of approach which delighted readers when his books started to appear.

In the couple of years immediately before signing on as a member of the crew of his first English ship, Conrad had been involved in some strange adventures in the south of France and in Spain, where it seems he had smuggled arms for the Royalist revolutionaries, but now there followed a long period spent at sea with only brief intervals in England. In the various British merchant ships in which he served, he started in the lowest rank, that of ordinary seaman, and he gradually climbed to the rank of captain. Most of these journeys took him to the East—to India, Australia and the East Indies, particularly the last, which furnished material for many of his best stories, including his first, *Almayer's Folly*. This first novel of his appeared in 1895, when he was thirty-seven, and was the result of some four years' labour in his leisure hours when at sea. The publishers to whom he sent it immediately recognised the work of this unknown writer to be that of a master in the art of story-telling. The encouragement he received from the public as well as the publishers led Conrad to give up his life of travel, and settle down to live quietly and cheaply in a small cottage in the south of England. Success as a writer later brought him large sums of money, but for nearly twenty years he had to live taking the greatest care to avoid expense, for he now had no other regular employment and, what is more, he had taken in 1896 the decisive step of marrying an English girl and starting a family. His marriage was a happy one, and this was to a great extent due to the common sense and devotion of his wife, who was younger by sixteen years. She provided the calm that Conrad lacked and the deep moral support that someone of his impulsive, artistic temperament so greatly needs.

Conrad was now a man of nearly forty. From then on till his death some thirty years later, Conrad's life was that of a hard-working writer, tied to his desk. It is unlikely that he found it easy to accept this change from endless travel; probably he had many moments of regret for the excitement and the beauty he had known in the Far East, for in the books that he now began to produce at regular intervals, there are nearly always many descriptions of the gorgeous scenery and also the picturesque people that contrasted in Conrad's mind so strongly with their other extremes, the office workers of London—in those days all dressed in black coats and top hats, and all seeming to want to be as like each other as possible. Whenever business called him to London, he would feel the desire to leave again as soon as he could. So it was natural for a man like Conrad to base his writing above all on his many personal memories of strange characters and exotic countries. His first books, which contain the memories that pressed foremost out of his mind, are perhaps his best, for they show what was most real and urgent for him to say. These are *Almayer's Folly* (1895), *An Outcast of the Islands* (1896), *The Nigger of the Narcissus* (1897), *Lord Jim* (1900), *Typhoon* (1903) and *Nostromo* (1904), and as can be seen from the dates of publication, one so close to another, they show his intensive output in these early years of his new career. His sales were not great, but he began to be recognised as a fine writer.

Nostromo stands separate from Conrad's main work in certain ways. Apart from the fact that the action takes place in South America, when his books are usually centred on Asia, Africa or the sea, there are other striking differences. In the first place, the story is a longer one than Conrad's previous books and the plot is more complicated. We feel that he has taken special trouble to produce a full-scale novel instead of the shorter type of work that perhaps suited him better and we also notice that the book is the result of deliberate construction rather than the natural overflow of his memories; it is less *personal*. But it is clear that Conrad felt the need to produce a work which would assure his position beside the other great English novelists of the nineteenth century; *Nostromo* is the result of this ambitious aim and it represents an unusual technical effort. It is probable that he himself felt that in his very first books, from *Almayer's Folly* on, he had said the best and most significant things he had to say, but without taking too much care. Now it was his job to continue to produce fiction, as it had become his career and he had to support a family, and he would have to avoid repeating himself in his themes.

In spite of all the trouble he had taken and the real value of the book, *Nostromo* long remained unappreciated by the public, although discerning critics had praised it. Conrad suffered deeply from this comparative failure; he spoke of the 'intense creative effort' he had made to write *Nostromo*. He himself was conscious that it was different from his other books, since he had worked on it, as he said, 'for twenty months, neglecting the common joys of life that fall to the lot of the humblest of this earth.' It was not until the publication of *Chance* in 1913 that Conrad achieved real success on a national scale.

Chance made him a rich man, instead of a poor struggling author who a year or two earlier had been deeply grateful to hear the news that he had been given a writer's pension of £100 a year. Strangely enough, *Chance* is not one of his best stories, but it was perhaps its success that encouraged him to write a better, *Victory* (1915). From then on till his death in 1924 Conrad continued to produce stories, but they are inferior to his best work.

If we try to assess Conrad's work as a novelist, we are bound to ask: What exactly is a novel? Or a short story? It may seem simple enough to say, but our answer really depends on what kinds we have read and on whether we are aware that these are literary forms that have gone through much development in the last two hundred years and are still changing. When we say, therefore, that Conrad was a great novelist, we have to add that he belonged to his time—the end of the nineteenth and the beginning of the twentieth centuries—and that his work represents only one side of the development of the English novel. The fact to remember is not that he was a foreigner, for his style was remarkably pure and he imposed himself without any difficulty as an English writer. His special quality lay in the experience of foreign lands and people that was the background of his early life, and this was something that appealed greatly to his first English readers. Conrad was able to offer them books that were descriptions of travel and real life, but which also had the human interest of fiction.

He did this at a time when British people were very conscious indeed of distant countries, for they had come suddenly to realise, at the end of the nineteenth century, that they had gathered round them an Empire which brought them into direct connection with all parts of the globe. And perhaps there was even a particularly strong interest in the East, which was, as we have seen, Conrad's speciality, for India had very many financial and commercial associations with Britain and, only shortly before, Queen Victoria had assumed the title of Empress of India. At the end of the reign, the celebration of her Golden and Diamond Jubilees, after fifty and then sixty years on the throne, brought attention more and more to the empire beyond the seas, for rulers and representatives came to London from all over the world, and, dressed in an endless variety of national costumes, were seen taking part in the processions to honour the Queen. This was just the moment that Conrad appeared with his enthusiastic descriptions of these distant parts.

At the beginning of his career as a sailor Conrad had changed from French to English ships. There was something significant in this, although he denied that it was anything more than chance, being merely due to passport difficulties at the time with the French authorities. But whatever the immediate cause of the move, Conrad never regretted it, for he very soon discovered he had a natural sympathy or affinity with the British. And as a result, his attitude towards his adopted country was always very positive and based on deep admiration. This naturally helped in the end to bring him success, for the British, like any other people, like to be liked and admired and the image of their character that Conrad held up to them in a mirror was not unflattering. Conrad had never lost his respect for the aristocratic virtues of heroism and courage which he had first known through his father and it seemed to him that these qualities were present particularly in the English sailors he worked with and in general in the people as a whole. If an Englishman had said this about his own compatriots, whether it was true or not, people would have not taken the same notice. That was one of the great advantages that Conrad had, as a foreign observer. And perhaps he did discover some important qualities in the British character, at least as it appeared at that time. For it was a period when, as we have said, the British nation displayed immense energy and determination. In Conrad's view, there was a further point in favour of the British—their political system and whole way of life was still distinctly aristocratic. This has changed almost totally since then, but Conrad would have found very distasteful the materialistic ideals of comfort and of a quiet life that seem now threatening to replace the old sense of adventure.

Not all Englishmen are sailors; nor are all the heroes of Conrad. But sailors do often develop the heroic qualities we have mentioned while they suffer inevitably from the lonely, hard life they lead. Here also was something that had a particular significance for Conrad—loneliness. In *Nostromo* as in nearly all his stories, we find the figure of a man standing apart or separated, for one reason or another, from his fellow-men. This was also a theme that could be understood by the British people of his time, for it was well known that to govern a vast Empire, men had to go out to remote corners where perhaps no other white man ever came and there they led a life of lonely struggle. Other writers as well as Conrad wrote of the problems of these people's lives—Rudyard Kipling and Somerset Maugham are perhaps the most famous. But again it was the special understanding of the observer from outside that made what Conrad had to say particularly interesting. He was not by any means all in favour of the white man; indeed he bitterly criticised their frequent greed and cruelty—stories such as *The Heart of Darkness* describe the wicked exploitation of Africans, and he showed that power, instead of making white men responsible, often made them mad.

Finally, there was one element in his stories that never failed to have a strong effect on his readers and this was his deep preoccupation with violence. This is a very modern preoccupation, for the problems of violence seem to be central to our age, and perhaps this is a reason for the interest that is still felt in Conrad's work. He himself displayed in his own life remarkable restlessness that expressed itself in sudden anger; his career was marked by many quarrels on the ships in which he sailed and later with the publishers for whom he wrote. There was even one incident of violence against himself when as a young man he tried to commit suicide. So all his stories have something to do with struggle, adventure or violence; and as long as these remain normal in human life, readers will not be lacking to show their interest in what Conrad has to say.

A note on the text

Nostromo was first published in 1904 by Harper and Brothers, London. It was republished in the Uniform Edition of the *Works* of Joseph Conrad, Dent, London, 1923–8, with an Author's Note to each volume. *Nostromo* was re-issued in the Collected Edition (volume 7), Dent, London, 1946–54. These Notes refer to pages in the Everyman Edition, Dent, London, 1957; 1966.

Part 2

Summaries

of NOSTROMO

A general summary

The scene is set in Costaguana, an imaginary South American republic on the west coast, during the last part of the nineteenth century. Nostromo is an Italian sailor who is employed in the port of Sulaco as overseer in charge of the handling of cargo. He rapidly becomes a respected local figure because of his efficiency, powers of leadership and general usefulness. He helps to save the President of the Republic who is being attacked by a mob.

In the hills behind Sulaco there is a very valuable silver mine, worked by a Concession that has been organised by an Englishman, Charles Gould, with financial aid obtained in the United States. It had always been considered that the silver of the mine brought a curse with it, but Gould's administration proved immensely successful. His wife, however, regretted that his whole life was swallowed up in his job. She devoted herself to works of charity and maintained their social position in the town; among their friends were Don José Avellanos, a respected statesman, and his daughter Antonia, who had both done much to support progressive elements in power.

A revolution, however, had overthrown the liberal-minded Dictator, who had been obliged to flee for his life from the town mob. Don José and his daughter took refuge in the woods, while Charles Gould made elaborate arrangements to defend the mine. He sent a vast quantity of silver away by sea in a small boat under the trusted Nostromo together with a young journalist, Martin Decoud, who was deeply in love with Antonia Avellanos. The boat had an accident and they saved the treasure with difficulty, hiding it on an uninhabited island outside the port of Sulaco.

Nostromo then returned to Sulaco in spite of danger and the presence of revolutionary troops. He let it be known that the treasure had been lost in the sea. Gould and his friends then sent Nostromo on a risky mission through enemy-occupied territory to fetch military aid. He was successful and the revolution was defeated in Sulaco and the surrounding district, which broke away from the capital of Costaguana and formed a new republic, able to progress rapidly with the backing of the fabulous riches of the mine.

Nostromo remained the sole person who knew the secret of the lost treasure, for his companion on the journey, Decoud, had committed suicide. A grave difficulty arose for him when a lighthouse was built on the island where the treasure lay. Nostromo solved this by arranging that an old Italian friend of his, Giorgio Viola, should be appointed keeper of the lighthouse, but a new complication came when Nostromo began a love affair with Viola's younger daughter, though he was officially engaged to be married to the elder girl. One night Viola shot and killed Nostromo by mistake, thinking he was somebody else trying to carry off his daughter. So the curse worked on Nostromo.

Detailed summaries

Part I: The silver of the mine. Chapter 1

The novel begins with a description of the harbour of Sulaco in the republic of Costaguana on the west coast of S. America. Called Golfo Placido because no strong wind ever disturbed it, the harbour has high mountains behind, but towards the sea lies the rocky, barren and uninhabited peninsula of Azuera that has an evil reputation, because it is said to contain great mineral wealth and to have caused the death of all those who have searched there. The harbour is nearly always covered on the mountain side by clouds and at night it is dark and swept by frequent rain. Outside the entrance to the harbour lie three small islands, the largest being only a mile long.

COMMENTARY: This description of the place and the history of Sulaco underlines their tragic, threatening quality. The rocks and the clouds have something frightening about them; so have the stories about men's failure to profit from the silver in the earth. Thus we have the right background for the tragic story that follows.

NOTES AND GLOSSARY

the last spur of the coast: the last point that stuck out into the sea

gringo: (*Spanish*) foreigner

mozo: (*Spanish*) young man

a sombre thunderhead . . . escapes into the offing: the dark head of a thundercloud moves across over the point of land

poncho: (*Spanish*) cloak made of thick wool

miradors: (*Spanish*) roof-tops

Chapter 2

The Oceanic Steam Navigation Company, known as the OSN, had built offices and a jetty for its ships, four of which had used it for many years on their regular coastal service. The company was respected for its reliability, largely due to the local superintendent, Captain Joseph Mitchell, who prided himself on his profound knowledge of the people and the country. The government of the republic was constantly changing hands and on one occasion Captain Mitchell had helped to save the life of an ex-dictator who was being pursued by a mob. The dictator had been taken away in one of the OSN boats while the mob had been defeated largely by the efforts of Nostromo, an Italian foreman employed by Captain Mitchell; his official title was Capataz de Cargadores. Nostromo had proved as able a leader of men in a fight as he was at work: he was much feared by all who knew him.

COMMENTARY: The reader is introduced to Nostromo and to Captain Mitchell, his employer. Mitchell is described as a pompous but honest man; in this chapter he is already used as a narrator—and this remains his main function in the book. We also see Nostromo at his most typical—as an inspired leader and man of action.

NOTES AND GLOSSARY

a tireless taskmaster: he was never tired of controlling the men under him and keeping them to their work

Chapter 3

A small hotel lay half-way between the harbour and the town, kept by Giorgio Viola with his wife and family. They were Italians and they looked after their compatriot Nostromo, whose absence they regretted when the rioting started. Giorgio, who had been a follower of Garibaldi in the battles for the independence of Italy, was a brave old man and, having barricaded his hotel, sat down with his rifle to await the mob and to defend his property as well as his frightened wife and two daughters.

COMMENTARY: We meet the Viola family in the hotel they run. Their dependence on Nostromo is shown. Giorgio Viola's firm character and his idealism as a follower of Garibaldi are stressed.

NOTES AND GLOSSARY

invoking the saint himself: calling on St John the Baptist for help

Nostromo: *nostro uomo*, Italian for 'our man'. The phrase used by Captain Mitchell was adopted as his name. Later (see Part III) he is known by his true name Fidanza

Garibaldi: Giuseppe Garibaldi (1807–82). Italian patriot and military leader in the struggles for the unification of Italy under the royal house of Savoy.

Chapter 4

Nostromo had not forgotten his friends while he had been fighting and having driven a part of the mob past the hotel, where they thought of making a stand, he came to the door and shouted to reassure the Viola family indoors, before continuing his pursuit towards the town. Viola's wife had been much frightened and was irritable, but she was a sick woman and had suffered from their life of wandering. Giorgio was much older than she, and had dedicated his life to the cause of liberty under Garibaldi with whom he had fought many battles both in South America, and later in Italy in the struggle for national independence. Now he had made his home in Sulaco where he was one of the most respected members of the colony of Italian workers, emigrants like himself, who often listened in the evening to his heroic stories of past battles.

COMMENTARY: We are given further details about the relationship between Nostromo and the Violas. Signora Teresa respects but cannot control him; she offers prayers for him and so do her children. We learn that Giorgio is an enemy to priests and a friend of the English.

NOTES AND GLOSSARY

Hola! Vecchio!: (*Italian*) Hullo! old man!

Avanti!: (*Italian*) Forward!

Signori inglesi: (*Italian*) the English gentlemen

Cavour: Casimir Cavour (1810–61). Italian statesman, associated with Garibaldi in the unification of Italy, but considered by Garibaldi to be a betrayer of the cause, as he compromised with the French

Aspromonte: battle in which Garibaldi and his followers had been defeated by the Piedmontese (1862)

Chapter 5

Eighteen months before the rioting, the Dictator had come south to Sulaco from the capital, in order to attend the ceremony that marked the beginning of the construction of the new railway. Captain Mitchell had presided over a great dinner on board one of the OSN boats and the chairman of the railway company had come from London. The Dictator, who was the leader of the conservative Blanco party, was in favour of the railway, but many of the great landowners in the southern province of Costaguana, although they supported his party, were against the new undertaking. At that time Nostromo was employed as camp-master with the railway engineers and he was given the special job of escorting the chairman, Sir John, on the last stage of his journey to Sulaco.

COMMENTARY: The theme of foreign financial interests is introduced, as we hear of the building of the railway, and its connection with the silver mine. We again meet Nostromo and see how his work is of such great value to his employers.

NOTES AND GLOSSARY

their own creature: the man whom they had put in power and who worked for them

diligencia: (*Spanish*) old-fashioned stagecoach drawn by horses

Chapter 6

Captain Mitchell had the very highest confidence in Nostromo, but exaggeratedly so, in the view of Dr Monygham, who spoke to his friend Mrs Gould on the subject. This English doctor was a bitter man, with little faith in human nature; Mrs Gould was one of the few people he respected. Mrs Gould was the wife of the owner of the San Tomé silver mine, Charles Gould, whose family had been established in Costaguana for three generations. The Goulds lived in one of the finest Spanish houses in Sulaco and Mrs Gould always was hospitable, especially in her welcome for the young mining engineers who came out to work under her husband.

Charles Gould (known to the local population by the Spanish name Don Carlos) had an extremely English appearance, but his family had long been associated in politics with the Costaguanero families of pure Spanish blood, who considered Charles one of themselves; Charles's uncle had been put to death by a former dictator belonging to the opposing political party. Charles's own views were impossible to discover; but his wife, who admired him so greatly, had seen that he combined English calm and a very practical mind with a true love of his second country. Their Spanish neighbour, Señor Avellanos, who visited them regularly, seemed to sense this too.

Mrs Gould had been a close witness of her husband's activity in the San Tomé mine, which he had inherited from his father when it was in a ruined state. His father, a very rich man, had been forced to accept ownership of the mine by the Government of his time, in return for a financial loan they needed. He had considered this almost a curse and had died a few years later as a result of worry caused by the mine. Charles Gould had spent his life putting the mine in order again and turning it into a very profitable enterprise once more, as it had been many years previously in the time when the Spanish had been masters of the country.

Mrs Gould had married when a young girl and she had arrived in Sulaco with her husband soon after the death of his father, Mr Gould senior. She had followed with enthusiasm Charles's successful efforts to re-activate the mine. Although he was sure of his own powers of management, he had needed considerable financial support which he found in the United States. Mr Holroyd, the millionaire from San Francisco who lent him the necessary capital, had been impressed by the young man's confidence but had warned him that if he began to fail, they would not continue to support him. Charles Gould was ready to accept these conditions; he was inspired by an intense desire to make a success out of the mine that had cast a shadow over his father's last years, even though his father had repeatedly told him never to get mixed up in the business that seemed to have a curse over it. Charles had seen that there was one danger, that he would have to use methods sometimes that were not strictly honest or legal, but he accepted this as a necessity. He had risked everything on his success.

COMMENTARY: This chapter gives a detailed introduction to Mr and Mrs Gould. We see how their married life has been dominated by Charles's one occupation, the development of the mine against which his father had warned him. The vital significance of Mr Holroyd's backing is shown and Conrad stresses the power and rather strange character of the millionaire.

NOTES AND GLOSSARY

a universal factotum: someone who does every kind of job needed

the Señor doctor: polite way of referring to the doctor in Spanish, Mr Doctor

Doña Emilia: Spanish term for lady, used in front of the Christian name; see also Don Carlos

Bolivar: Simon Bolivar (1783–1830). Political leader and General who drove the Spanish out of Venezuela and Colombia, and who came close to uniting all the Latin South American republics

wear his heart on his sleeve: express all his emotions openly

would decline to discuss them: used gently to refuse

patio: (*Spanish*) inner courtyard of Spanish house

philtres: magic drinks

maw: the stomach of a large animal, thus meaning a hole that swallows up everything that is thrown into it

pronunciamentos: (*Spanish*) political proclamations published by the head of any revolutionary party

versed in the ways of Governments: he knew all about the habits, good and bad, of Governments

concession-holder: one who is authorised by the Government to use some privilege or property, here to exploit the silver mine
iniquitous: wicked (a strong word of condemnation)
Creole: of Spanish blood, born in South America
accessible character someone who is ready to listen
redress: justice for wrong that has been done
the mantle has descended on her: she had inherited the task and the authority that went with it
a real hustler: a man who pushes people till he gets things done
tawdriness: cheap and vulgar quality
drawers of water and hewers of wood: servants who do all the hard work
an air of breeding a look of refinement
even the most legitimate touch of materialism was wanting: she did not have even that small interest in material things which is quite permissible
a game . . . worth the candle: something worth the effort
temperament of a Puritan: very serious, disapproving of pleasure, believing in hard work
redemption of the mine: buying the mine back, that is, getting it out of debt and becoming full owner of it
persona non grata: (*Latin*) person not welcome (a phrase used by governments when requiring a foreigner to leave the country)
a stiff upper lip: ability to conceal one's unhappiness
throw good money after bad: go on wasting money on something that has proved unsuccessful

Chapter 7

Don José Avellanos always praised Charles for his patriotic spirit, and his wife too. She had accompanied Charles on his expeditions made to the interior of the country with the object of recruiting workers for the mine, and she had got to know Costaguana well. The native population of peasants had always been exploited and downtrodden; patient passivity was their most striking characteristic.

Charles always made sure that he would be able to count on the support of those in power; by paying heavy bribes he had obtained, whenever necessary, written authorisation from the local governors of the province of Sulaco; but he did not make friends with these men whom he bribed and they did not react well to his air of silent superiority. It was known also that he was in regular contact with the government of the capital; an important lawyer there was pointed out as the political agent of the San Tomé mine and private correspondence between him and Charles was by means of a discreet mule-driver who travelled frequently over the mountains for this purpose.

COMMENTARY: The author gives us details of some of Charles's problems, particularly how he has to buy protection for his mine from corrupt politicians.

NOTES AND GLOSSARY

mozos de campo:	(*Spanish*) farm workers
calzoneras:	(*Spanish*) button-down trousers
pueblos:	(*Spanish*) villages
potreros:	(*Spanish*) fields of pasture
camino real:	(*Spanish*) the Royal road
alcaldes:	(*Spanish*) mayors
fiscales:	(*Spanish*) tax collectors
drew the line:	he would not go as far as that.

Chapter 8

Sulaco has changed since the time of the story. Now the town lives under modern conditions, the streets and railway have been vastly extended and the workers in the port show their discontent by serious labour troubles. But Nostromo in his day never allowed anything of that sort and after a holiday, when his workers had drunk too much, he would personally go round the town in the early dawn, collecting them by force and the threat of his revolver.

The San Tomé mine attracted workers by offering them protection against injustice; the police treated more carefully the men who wore the special colours of the mine, green and white. They lived in organised village communities near the mine under the strict control of Don Pépé, a retired army officer, who although of humble origin, had pronounced political views that recommended him to the Blanco Party aristocrats. When in town, he was a regular visitor to the Aristocratic Club of Sulaco, as well as to the Goulds' drawing-room, where his simple loyalty and military efficiency were always honoured. He knew all the hundreds of mine workers by name and supervised their attendance at work and the security of the camp by night; he was proud of his unofficial title which he fully deserved—El Señor Gobernador—the Governor. The English doctor and a Spanish priest, Father Roman, were also living up at the mine.

The mining community in fact was so well organised that it brought a sense of security to the whole neighbourhood; they were left alone by the authorities and for Charles Gould this was enough for the moment.

One of the first changes had been the drying-up of the waterfall near the mine, for the water was needed for the turbines that were situated in the valley below. The turbines worked the stamps that formed the silver into ingots. Once the silver was ready, it was despatched under escort down to the port, before being sent off by boat. The escort was large and heavily armed and rode at a gallop, for many robberies were carried out in the country of a very daring nature, particularly under the leadership of a famous army deserter, Hernandez, who terrorised all rich travellers. But it was said that even some of his band had now joined the guards of the mine which had become such a great power in the land.

Above all, the rumour spread that the reforming government of the dictator Ribiera had been helped to power by the San Tomé administration. When this rumour reached the ears of Sir John, the English chairman of the railway, he was encouraged to believe that the country was moving towards stability and deserved the heavy financial support he himself was proposing to give.

On the occasion of the dinner to celebrate the starting of work on the railway, Sir John had been given the greatest honour after the President-Dictator himself, thus causing annoyance to the brutal-minded Provincial Governor, General Montero. The dinner gave Mrs Gould an opportunity to get Sir John to promise that the hotel belonging to old Viola should not be disturbed, although it was situated on a part of land bought for the construction of the railway. Delighted by this news, Viola was quick to communicate it to Nostromo, who appeared just then, dressed in his finest costume for the public celebrations. Nostromo looked imposing and attracted attention wherever he went; a circle formed round him when a pretty young dark-skinned girl came up and claimed a present from him as her lover. He gave her the splendid silver buttons from his coat. By then the visit of the President-Dictator Ribiera was over, for his ship was steaming out of harbour, saluted by guns. The next time he came was a year-and-a-half later, as a hunted refugee, and it was then that Nostromo saved him from the attacking mob. Shortly after this, Nostromo was caught up in a further unfortunate drama.

COMMENTARY: The development of the organisation of the mine is explained; the idea of its increasing economic value to the country is stressed, and we turn back again (p.116) to a description of the dinner on board the OSN ship, with further reference to Sir John and to General Montero. The first part of the novel ends with Mitchell's remark about the later history of Nostromo. Thus this chapter looks both backward and forward, and helps to bind the novel together.

NOTES AND GLOSSARY

pulperia: (*Spanish*) country tavern
in a stentorian voice: very loudly
a fellow in a thousand: a quite exceptional fellow
lanceros: (*Spanish*) lancers, soldiers
Holy Office: the Roman Catholic Inquisition, founded to combat heresy
bullion epaulettes: gold decoration on shoulders of officer's uniform
el Señor Gobernador: (*Spanish*) the Governor
banteringly: in a joking but friendly manner
shifts: sets of workers, working each for a given number of hours
screeners and ore-breakers: workers who break up and separate the metal
flumes: channels down which water is directed
nooks and crannies: all the hidden corners
corrida: (*Spanish*) bull fight
posada: (*Spanish*) inn
small fry: unimportant people
padre: (*Spanish*) priest
spiritual and temporal pastors: those who look after them, spiritually and in a material sense
uncanny: of a strange, unexplained and slightly frightening nature
legionary: soldier of ancient Rome
bituminous: covered with bitumen, a tar-like substance
muy linda e maravillosa: (*Spanish*) very pretty
yerba: (*Spanish*) herbs
posadero: (*Spanish*) inn-keeper
blockhouse: a small square building with very thick walls built for defence
Moreno: (*Spanish*) dark-skinned man
their worships: title of respect given to the Caballeros (gentlemen)
retort: part of the furnace for purifying the silver
muchachos: (*Spanish*) young men
salteadores: (*Spanish*) highway-robbers
burros: (*Spanish*) donkeys
macaques: (*Spanish*) rascals
Jefe: (*Spanish*) chief
sanguinary: bloody (here used as swearword)
imperium in imperio: (*Latin*) an empire within an empire, in other words an independent government
in the thick of things: in the centre of what was going on and knowing about everything

a shore billet: accommodation on land
marked an epoch: was of historical importance
Winchester: a fast-firing rifle
leperos: (*Spanish*) lower-class people
Caramba: (*Spanish*) exclamation of astonishment
brazen-faced scramble: a battle that was fought for openly selfish motives
occult influence: secret and of supernatural power
invested with a mandate of reform: given power with a programme of reform
backwoods hero: the soldier who came from humble origins in the country
vaquero: (*Spanish*) cowherd
accredited to the Court of St James: Ambassador in London
Hear! Hear!: phrase of approval
maté: (*Spanish*) a type of South American tea
padrona: (*Spanish*) mistress, of a house or hotel
serape: (*Spanish*) shawl
buon viaggio: (*Italian*) have a good journey!
morenita: (*Spanish*) dark-skinned girl
querido: (*Spanish*) dear
thee: accusative form of 'thou', to show the use of the familiar form of 'you' in the Spanish

Part II: The Isabels. Chapter 1

The civil war that broke out had not interrupted the activity of the mine. Indeed, the whole northern province formed by the country round Sulaco, cut off by the high mountains, had remained undisturbed. Don José Avellanos had made great efforts to gather support for Ribiera as candidate for the Presidency, as a man who seemed to offer for the first time a true promise of progress and reform. Don José's own past, and his long sufferings as a prisoner of the earlier cruel dictatorship of Guzman Bento, made him widely respected, and politicians in the capital were willing to follow his lead, especially as he was known to command material support through the San Tomé mine. For Charles Gould, in his correspondence with Mr Holroyd, his great financial backer in California, had got him to agree that Ribiera should be supported. Thus Don José felt great gratitude towards the Goulds.

COMMENTARY: This chapter provides a short summary of the political background, mentioning Don José and his opposition to the previous dictator, Guzman Bento, as well as the influence of Gould which had been used to support the progressive Ribiera Government.

NOTES AND GLOSSARY

morse apparatus: a machine for sending telegraphic messages by means of the morse code, a system of dots and dashes, or short and long sounds, representing letters and numerals, invented by Samuel Morse (1791–1872)

a byword: well-known

Inquisitor: member of the Catholic Inquisition

benighted aristocrat: left over from the past and abandoned

el Gobierno Supremo: (*Spanish*) the Supreme Governor

factions: small quarrelling parties

swashbuckler: vulgar adventurer

inviolable sanctuary: (holy space) a room into which no one might enter and disturb him

Chapter 2

Ribiera had been elected President-Dictator and had been given a free hand in a 'Five-Year Mandate'. Don José hoped that this would bring reforms and new life—or what he called 'regeneration'—to the country. Ribiera had made a mistake in appointing as War Minister the brother of General Montero, the military hero of the day and already Governor of Sulaco. Unfortunately both brothers proved to be traitors and brought out the army in revolt against the Government.

Sulaco was cut off from the capital Santa Marta by the rebels, but protected by the mountains; it was active under Don José in producing men and money to go to the defence of the legitimate government. His patriotism was an inspiration to the whole province and even Hernandez the bandit had offered his help in return for a pardon—the very conditions which the rebels themselves had proposed in order to gain his support. The troops that usually garrisoned Sulaco left by OSN steamer to go south to fight and they were given an enthusiastic 'send off' from the harbour; all the best families came in their coaches and the commander General Barrios boasted in front of Mrs Gould that in three weeks he would have captured the rebel General Montero and be able to display him in a cage to the public. Don José was also present; he had, as chairman of a recently formed Patriotic Committee, been responsible for obtaining modern rifles from Europe for the troops, though nobody knew how much these arms were paid for by the local families and how much by the secret funds from abroad that Don José was believed to control. Sitting with Don José in Mrs Gould's carriage was his daughter, Antonia Avellanos, who as her father's only child, was his closest companion and assistant in all his political struggles.

She had been brought up in Europe and much to everybody's scandal took no notice of the usual rigid Spanish-American conventions with regard to an unmarried girl's behaviour.

COMMENTARY: The new civil war started by the Montero brothers is described, with the reactions in Sulaco that follow.

NOTES AND GLOSSARY

Nestor: wise old man, from the ancient Greek hero

ex-guerrillero: (*Spanish*) the former guerrilla soldier

oracularly: in a phrase that gives the meaning without using precise names

regeneration: rebirth, through reform

fastness: secure position of defence

send-off: ceremony of good-bye

landau: a large open carriage drawn by two horses

Chapter 3

Antonia's attention was turned towards an elegantly dressed young man of handsome appearance, by name Martin Decoud, godson of her father. He came from a distinguished Creole family—of Spanish blood but born in Costaguana—that had long been settled in Europe. He had worked in Paris as newspaper correspondent and obtained for himself a rather undeserved reputation as an expert journalist, for he did not take his job very seriously. He had surprised both himself and all who knew him, by agreeing to negotiate the purchase of arms on behalf of the Sulaco Patriotic Committee. He had also unexpectedly decided to travel with the previous rifles to Costaguana to deliver them. His family immediately saw that this journey was connected with his interest in Antonia, with whom he had fallen in love some years previously when she had been in Paris. Don José had welcomed him enthusiastically as a returning patriot and had persuaded him to undertake the job of editing a newspaper in the province of Sulaco, intended to combat Montero's propaganda which was making disturbing appeals to the people to rise against the rich families that governed with the aid of foreign money.

COMMENTARY: Martin Decoud is introduced; he is shown as an intelligent man whose attitude in politics is largely influenced by his personal feelings rather than principles.

NOTES AND GLOSSARY

creole: of Spanish blood, born in South America

boulevardier: (*French*) a man who wasted his time walking up and down the Paris boulevards

blague: (*French*) joke
opera-bouffe: (*French*) comic opera
une farce macabre: (*French*) a frightening and terrible game of pretence
un grotesque vaniteux et féroce: (*French*) a ridiculous fellow who was both vain and ferocious
connaissait la question à fond: (*French*) understood the question thoroughly
une bonne blague, hein?: (*French*) a good joke, what?
c'est funambulesque!: (*French*) it is quite absurd!
blabbing to our Chargé d'Affaires: telling the secret to our Government's representative
familias principales: (*Spanish*) most important families
Pro Patria: (*Latin*) for the sake of the fatherland
paraliticos: (*Spanish*) paralysed, that is, useless, inactive people
Porvenir: (*Spanish*) name chosen for Decoud's newspaper—it means the Future
august calling: an ironical way of expressing a very important task in life.

Chapter 4

General Barrios gave the appearance of having drunk rather too much as he boasted to Mrs Gould and the other Europeans present that he would shortly bring back Montero in a cage. Barrios, a son of the people, was a brave and popular soldier whose defect in private life was a mania for gambling which left him constantly short of money; but he could be counted upon as a loyal general even though he was said to be unlucky in battle. It was evident that some of his listeners had little respect for the departing general. But Mrs Gould heroically concealed her disappointment; she had begun to understand her husband's attitude better now, for he had long refused to discuss the unsatisfactory leaders of his country.

Mrs Gould took Don José, Antonia and Decoud back with her in her carriage and stopped on the way to exchange a few words with Viola outside his hotel. The old Italian clearly did not have much belief in the fighting quality of the troops that were leaving, but he had words of praise for their rifles that pleased Don José. Decoud was in a bad mood and annoyed first Viola and then the others in the carriage by his cynical and questioning attitude. But Don José refused to admit any lack of confidence in Barrios as the carriage drove back to the Goulds' house in town.

COMMENTARY: Decoud's cynicism is contrasted with the ignorance of General Barrios and the naivety of the young English engineer. Don

José's idealism is shown as being joined to experience and a certain mature wisdom.

NOTES AND GLOSSARY

embustero: (*Spanish*) liar
tolderia: (*Spanish*) primitive Indian house
monte: (*Spanish*) game of cards used for gambling
il manque de tenue: (*Spanish*) he does not know how to behave correctly
Ferro Carril: (*Spanish*) railway
picardia: (*Spanish*) trick
the strain was telling on him: the prolonged tension was beginning to affect his health
le sort en est jeté: (*French*) the die is cast, that is, the decision has been taken
a la casa: (*Spanish*) drive home!
her protégé: the man whose interests she was protecting
another title to his regard: another reason for his respecting her
bersaglieri: (*Italian*) Italian infantry soliders famous for their very rapid way of marching
esclavos: (*Spanish*) slaves
the Great Pompey: English name for Cnæus Pompeius, a Roman General (107–48BC) who joined with Julius Caesar and Crassus in forming the first triumviate in 60BC but soon became Caesar's rival and enemy. Caesar defeated him at the battle of Pharsalia in Greece, after which Pompey took refuge in Egypt but was assassinated there
Pharsalia: the battle in Greece in which Pompey was finally defeated, 48BC
vir Romanus: (*Latin*) Roman man
licked once for all: completely and finally defeated
gone to pot: gone to ruin
the hour of Oracion: (*Spanish*) the time of evening prayer
sombreros and rebozos: (*Spanish*) hats and scarves

Chapter 5

Decoud continued to express his discontent and began to speak of the way the country was exploited by foreigners, which Mrs Gould interpreted as a reference to her husband. But Don José took no notice of his remarks and quietly reminded Decoud that he must publish the news of the despatch of the troops in a way that would gain the maximum moral effect both in the country and abroad. Decoud found himself forced by his love for Antonia to act on behalf of a cause in which he only half believed. He said to himself that he was not a patriot, but a lover.

In the drawing-room of the Goulds' house, Don José put on a confident tone of voice as he talked enthusiastically to Charles Gould about the departing troops and their new rifles. Meanwhile Antonia and Decoud were having a long conversation standing in one of the tall windows looking on to the street. Antonia was taking no notice of the usual conventions by talking so publicly with Decoud who was not even officially engaged to be married to her. Decoud reminded her that for her sake he had, by his work on the newspaper, made himself a man marked for certain death if Montero were victorious. She said some words of true sympathy which he had not expected. Passionately he suggested they should leave the country that was so mismanaged. Why had Montero not simply been bribed? That was the usual thing to do, and it should have been possible. But since that opportunity had been lost, he proposed another idea—that the province of Sulaco should declare itself separate, as it was easily rich enough to support itself, and return to their original policy of Federalism in Costaguana. The province would be known as the Occidental Republic. Above all, he refused to believe in patriotism for this country where the word was used merely to cover crimes of lawlessness.

But he could not alter Antonia's idealism and her loyalty to her father's views. He began talking instead about her uncle, the grand-vicar of the Cathedral, whom they saw coming to the house. Padre Corbelán was a fanatic priest and missionary, who had a certain softness for Decoud whom he called a 'heathen'. It was known that Corbelán took part in politics and had used Nostromo to take messages to Hernandez the bandit, but the police did not want to take action against him—not because of his position as a priest but because he was the brother-in-law of Don José.

One of the last guests to leave the reception at the Goulds' was a German-Jewish merchant, Mr Hirsch. He wished for assistance in exporting animal hides and he also had thought that he could sell Charles Gould dynamite from Germany; but Charles showed clearly that he was not interested in hides and, as for dynamite, he said he had enough in the mine to blow up the whole of Sulaco. It was obvious from what he said that he intended to resist by force any attempt to take the mine out of the hands of the Gould Concession.

COMMENTARY: Decoud's political position is summed up in his words: 'No one is a patriot for nothing' (p.189). The reception in Gould's drawing-room serves to concentrate the reader's attention on the political interests that are involved, including that of the Church and the Government, but Charles Gould himself and the power of the mine are central to everything.

NOTES AND GLOSSARY

morions and corselets: ancient types of armour to protect the body
sala: (*Spanish*) large room
quelle farce!: (*French*) what an absurd game!
novio: (*Spanish*) young man, official suitor of a girl
you snubbed me: you made me feel inferior
Charlotte Corday: Charlotte Corday (1768–93) was a young French girl who, in the name of liberty, killed the revolutionary leader Marat in his bath and was herself guillotined in punishment.
par exemple!: (*French*) what a thing to say!
would get even with me: have this revenge on me
gran' bestia: (*Spanish*) monster (literally a 'great beast')
Intrada de la Sombra: (*Spanish*) entrance to the shady side (of the bull ring where seats are divided into those in the sun and those in the shade)
loafing: standing and sitting about, wasting one's time
Rey de Sulaco: (*Spanish*) King of Sulaco
brazeros: (*Spanish*) braziers, small cooking stoves
esprit fort: (*French*) disbeliever in the Church, who takes no notice of religious rules
fandango: (*Spanish*) Spanish dance
soutane: (*French*) cassock, long dress worn by priest
proselytes: followers, people who could be converted to his faith
despoiled Church: the Church had lost its lands and property because they had been taken over by the State
paramos: (*Spanish*) heaths, wild country
what would you have?: (phrase not really used in English, but used by Conrad to reproduce the Spanish construction) what can one do?
the sequestrated Dominican Convent: the Convent had been suppressed by the State and allowed to fall into ruin
find the authorities with their boots off: the Government would be unprepared
c'est trop beau: (*French*) it (the report) is too good
wrong-headedness: obstinacy in doing the wrong thing
dementia: (*Latin*) madness
peons: (*Spanish*) poor agricultural labourers
cringing: over-humbly trying to please
quebrada: (*Spanish*) gorge or ravine
portended a failure: was a sign to him that failure was likely
holding on like grim death: holding on to what one has got, in spite of every difficulty

Chapter 6

When Charles was left alone with his wife, he told her that he had arranged to bring down the latest supply of silver from the mine to the harbour early the next morning. As they talked, it became clear that she was sad and tired of the life they led with all the doubtful compromises they were forced to make for the sake of the mine. But he repeated his old phrase 'There is no going back now', and she realised that nothing would make him stop.

Mrs Gould left the room and found that Decoud had returned, on the pretence that he was looking for Antonia's fan, but really to tell her privately that there was bad news. The Ribierists had been defeated in a big battle; the only hope, according to Decoud, lay in the province of Sulaco separating from the rest of Costaguana. He explained openly to Mrs Gould that it was only his love for Antonia that made him intend to stay and that he had no choice but to continue opposing Montero who would certainly have him killed if he gained possession of Sulaco. He had spoken to Nostromo who had promised that he and his men would support the Europeans if there was trouble in the town as Mrs Gould was afraid there might be, especially when the news of Montero's victory became known. Mrs Gould's heart was heavier than ever before, as she thought of the silver that had gradually turned her husband away from his original pure inspiration in life.

COMMENTARY: Decoud's discussion of separatism for Sulaco prepares the later part of the story, but perhaps the most significant moment in this chapter comes with his analysis of Charles's character (pp.214–5). Thus Conrad again stresses Charles's idealism, even though it may be misguided.

NOTES AND GLOSSARY

amigo: (*Spanish*) friend, a term here addressed to the servant

canard: (*French*) a false rumour

Non, Madame. Rien n'est perdu: (French) No, Madam. Nothing is lost.

hijo del pais: (*Spanish*) son of the country

rather carried away: my feelings have made me say more than I intended

muy bien: (*Spanish*) very good

heard no end of tales: heard endless stories

circumvallation: (an unusual, technical word) rampart or wall of earth round an area to be defended

Chapter 7

Decoud was writing a long letter, to his sister in Paris, as he sat in Viola's hotel close to the harbour. It was dark night outside but the Italian workmen had lighted fires by the railway line that they were guarding. Decoud began by describing the riot that had taken place in the town and how Nostromo had saved the President of the Republic from the mob with the aid of his own 'cargadores' or lightermen. Meanwhile the Europeans had driven off the drunken crowd by firing from the windows of their club into the main square. Decoud knew that the principal object of the riot was to get hold of the silver from the San Tomé mine which had been stored in the Custom House in the harbour. Two Deputies of the Provincial Assembly, by name Gamacho and Fuentes, had put themselves at the head of the mob, having decided to go over to the cause of Montero when they had heard the news of the victory.

Decoud was extremely tired, for he had not slept for some forty hours, but he went on writing as he felt a great need to send a message, perhaps his last, to his sister. He described how Viola's wife was dying upstairs in a room above him and everything was silent.

The previous day he had witnessed a meeting in the Goulds' house of the last remaining members of the Provincial Assembly who had not already fled from the town. Decoud had tried to put some courage into them and inspire them with his own idea of separating from the rest of the country. But he could see that they had decided in advance on unresisting surrender to Montero whenever he should arrive. Decoud therefore had concentrated on presenting his plan for separation to the only people who counted—Charles Gould and his wife. The news had meanwhile come that Pedro Montero and his men had crossed the mountains unexpectedly and were on their way to Sulaco, where they would probably arrive within two days. Decoud had encouraged the Goulds to secure the safety of the latest supply of silver, already stored at the harbour, by sending it out of the country at once. Decoud and Nostromo would take it by boat. Antonia was looking after her father, who was clearly dying, broken by the shock of the news that meant the end of all his work.

As he finished writing the letter to his sister, Decoud fell asleep but was soon woken up by the arrival of Nostromo. The dying wife of Viola from her bed upstairs sent for Nostromo and begged him to fetch a priest for her; but Nostromo refused, knowing that he had no time, as it was very urgent that he should leave with the silver. Full of rage, she predicted that he would get nothing from this work but poverty and starvation. But Nostromo hurried away after making his last arrangements with Viola in case he never returned.

Soon afterwards, Nostromo and Decoud steered the lighter full of silver out of the harbour; it was as usual an extremely dark night, so that only lucky instinct was sufficient to guide Nostromo. As the wind was inadequate, they had to row, but Decoud, very tired and unaccustomed to rowing, suffered cruelly. Nostromo grumbled to him about the responsibility he had undertaken, but Decoud could see that his pride in himself would carry him through, whatever happened, even though he had not been told what reward he might receive.

But quite soon, they made an unfortunate discovery—somebody was hiding in the boat. In the darkness they dragged out a man that they recognised as Señor Hirsch, the hide merchant who had visited Charles Gould. He gave no sign of life but he was obviously not dead.

COMMENTARY: The novelist uses Decoud as a supplementary narrator (after Mitchell) by making him write a long letter to his sister, describing the dramatic events of the riot. A significant link between Decoud and Nostromo is shown (p.246); both are actors who are not entirely convinced of the importance of the events into which they have been drawn. Their departure at night with the silver is perhaps the central point of the story.

NOTES AND GLOSSARY

Feudalism: political and economic system of Mediaeval Europe, here standing as a symbol of the past that must be destroyed

shambles: a slaughter-house where animals are killed; here, a place full of blood

camerista: (*Spanish*) lady's maid

whom I exposed in Paris, where he tried to pass himself off for . . .: whose trick I revealed to the public, for he tried to pretend that he was . . .

Duc de Morny: The Duke (1811–65) was a brother of Napoleon III of France, whose rise to power he shared

junta: (*Spanish*) small group in government, council of state

conclave: secret meeting

soeur chérie: (*French*) dearest sister

in the small hours: in the hours immediately after midnight

quien sabe?: (*Spanish*) who knows?

felucca: type of small sailing ship

he laid no money by: he saved no money

adios, viejo: (*Spanish*) good-bye, old man

por Dios!: (*Spanish*) by God!

gunwale: side of the boat

propitiated his companion: said what was necessary to keep him happy

Chapter 8

Nostromo suggested throwing Hirsch into the sea; this made him show signs of life quite quickly and he told his story. He had tried to escape from the riot by seeking refuge in the harbour and finally hidden in the lighter that held the silver, though he now regretted it as he saw what a desperate adventure he was mixed up in. He was in great fear and rushed to obey Nostromo when he ordered him to lie down in the fore-part of the boat. He was obviously a coward who could cause trouble by hysterical behaviour in time of danger.

The breeze was very slight and the boat moved very slowly. Suddenly they heard the noise of an approaching steamer which stopped very close to them, invisible in the darkness as it carried no lights, which made Nostromo conclude that it was full of soldiers. In a whisper he told Decoud that he would sink the lighter immediately if Hirsch revealed their position by making any sound, or shrieking, as he might easily do in the madness of his fear.

As Nostromo guessed, Sotillo, the military commandant of Esmeralda, was in the steamer, bringing troops to capture the treasure. Before the recent revolution, he had frequented the Goulds' house in Sulaco and had seemed a loyal supporter of the Ribiera government; he had also paid marked attention to Antonia Avellanos, by marrying whom he thought to get closer to the Gould Concession and its immense wealth. Sotillo was not aware of the latest developments of the situation in Sulaco; he did not know that there had been riots, or that the President had escaped and been pursued by Montero's brother. Sotillo had simply taken over a government steamer that was lying in the harbour at Esmeralda and brought his troops down the coast under cover of darkness. There had been a quarrel between one of his officers and the captain; it was this that had caused the boat to stop. The second time it stopped was because they were searching for the Isabels, the group of islands at the mouth of the harbour that would show them where they were. Nostromo guessed that this was what they intended and hoped that, however close the steamer passed, they would not notice the lighter.

The steamer, however, struck the lighter in its course, with a heavy sideways blow. Señor Hirsch let out a piercing scream; the anchor of the steamer became entangled with the lighter's mast and as it passed him, Hirsch caught hold of the anchor and went on shouting for help as the steamer continued on its way. He was soon rescued and taken before Sotillo who realised that they had run down some small boat but refused to accept the idea that they might have also sunk the treasure they were hurrying to capture.

So, by a miracle, Nostromo and Decoud escaped with the lighter that had just survived the blow. They took the boat, which was already leaking heavily, to the closest and largest island of the Isabels, where they hid the treasure before dawn. Decoud remained on the island, hoping to be able to join the next mail boat that passed. Meanwhile Nostromo took the empty lighter back in the direction of the mainland, and, sinking it before he reached the harbour, got to the shore by swimming.

COMMENTARY: The discovery of Hirsch, the collision with Sotillo's steamer and the burial of the treasure on the island form a dramatic chapter that moves forward faster than any previous part of the novel.

NOTES AND GLOSSARY

quien vive?:	(*Spanish*) who goes there? (literally, who lives?), a phrase used by soldiers on guard
overweening vanity:	excessive vanity
painter:	a rope attached to a small boat
que picardia!:	(*Spanish*) what a trick!
su merced:	(*Spanish*) your honour! your worship!
è vero!:	(*Spanish*) it is true
dinghy:	(*Spanish*) small boat
matreros:	(*Spanish*) cattle-thieves
calabozo:	(*Spanish*) prison

Part III: The Lighthouse. Chapter 1

After having helped to load the silver on the boat, the European workmen in the employment of the railway were withdrawn from the harbour by their chief engineer, who did not wish to be further involved in any action that might spoil his position of political neutrality; this was particularly necessary now that representatives of the Monterist régime were expected to arrive in Sulaco any hour, both by sea and from over the mountains.

Dr Monygham, who had been attending Viola's wife at the hotel, had a conversation with the engineer when he passed that way. The doctor expressed his disapproval of the sending-away of the silver and also showed pessimism about the chances of success for Decoud's separatism. He also blamed Nostromo for having made the state of Viola's wife worse by something he had said or done.

COMMENTARY: The discussion between the engineer and Dr Monygham brings out the doctor's character and his intelligence; he suggests that Viola's wife was in a way in love with Nostromo and, more important, that Nostromo has so far not been rewarded by any special material advantage in spite of his remarkable services.

NOTES AND GLOSSARY

give our rulers a handle against the railway: give them something which they can criticise us for

tramposo: (*Spanish*) cheat

oligarchs: a word of Greek origin, meaning rulers, when the government is in the hands of a few

Chapter 2

The honest old sailor in charge of the steamship service, Captain Mitchell, had stayed on the wharf of the harbour after the lighter full of silver had put to sea. When the steamer with Sotillo and his troops arrived in the night, Captain Mitchell had, out of curiosity, simply remained standing in a dark corner to witness the disembarkation. Unfortunately he was caught and taken roughly before Sotillo who had made his headquarters in the harbour Customs House. Sotillo recognised him and decided to treat him in a friendly way, though Mitchell's violent protests at his arrest made him change his tone, especially when the old sailor refused to give any information about the silver. Mitchell was thrown into a dark cell and was soon joined by Dr Monygham whom Sotillo's troops had also found and arrested.

COMMENTARY: The arrest of Mitchell and the doctor leads to the misunderstanding that the silver has been sunk, as well as Nostromo and Decoud drowned.

NOTES AND GLOSSARY

guileless: innocent, incapable of any trick to deceive

in the thick of things: see glossary for p.112

mi teniente!: (*Spanish*) my lieutenant! (phrase used when speaking to officer of that rank)

to make head or tail of it: to make any sense out of a story

to collect such few wits as remained to him: to enable him to think again

hochwohlgeborene herren: (*German*) respected sirs

inconceivableness of this experience: the impossibility of imagining that such a thing could happen

wanting in the misty idealism of the Northerners: who do not have the vague idealism of Northern peoples

I am up to your tricks!: I am not deceived by you

picaro: (*Spanish*) man who plays tricks, cheat

bosh: nonsense (a slang word)

get wind of the affair: hear of what was happening

Chapter 3

Both men were released after a few hours, but the Doctor, for reasons of his own, offered to help Sotillo to discover what had been done with the silver. Sotillo's plans had already changed since his arrival for he had learnt from the railway engineer about Pedro Montero's approach over the mountains and this was news to him; as a result he decided not to occupy the town straightaway. This would leave time, as the engineer hoped, for many more people to take refuge outside Sulaco, in the woods of Los Hatos, where the bandit Hernandez, now appointed general, was ready to protect all those who fled from the new Montero régime. Many went, including the dying Don José Avellanos and his daughter Antonia.

COMMENTARY: Dr Monygham's decision to deceive Sotillo is important, as it begins the process whereby he regains self-respect. Gould and Hernandez the bandit are shown as two men whose will-power leads them to decisive action, independent of normal legality.

NOTES AND GLOSSARY

a put-up job on the part of Gould: an arrangement by Gould to deceive everyone

chummy: friendly with each other ('chum' is schoolboys' slang for friend)

beachcomber: a worthless idler

hobbling gait: irregular, uneven step (caused by the doctor's feet having been deformed by torture)

he ignored the doctor pointedly: he showed clearly that he was not going to take any notice of him

suavely: in a calm and persuasive tone

as a drowning man catches at a straw: welcomed the idea as their salvation

llaneros: (*Spanish*) plainsmen

carretas: (*Spanish*) covered carts

sereno: (*Spanish*) watchman

compadre: (*Spanish*) companion

put a price upon his head: offered a reward for his capture

by the same precarious tenure: by the same right, not very strongly established

debasing contacts [of the lawlessness of the land]: the absence of law meant that everyone was corrupted

partida: (*Spanish*) departure

Chapter 4

Charles Gould had accompanied Avellanos and his daughter part of the way, and on his return home he found certain members of the Political Assembly who were already preparing an official welcome to Pedro Montero when he arrived as the new Governor. Gould refused to associate himself with this welcome, thus making it clear that he would not lend the name of the San Tomé mine as a protection; indeed he had privately decided that he would use dynamite to destroy the mine utterly rather than allow it to be taken over by this latest revolution.

Dr Monygham arrived with the incorrect news of the loss of silver and the drowning of Decoud and Nostromo—which was what he had heard through Sotillo. Gould now felt that he was being pushed more and more by circumstances into the only course of action that could save the mine, in other words—support for Decoud's separatist plan.

COMMENTARY: This chapter is to be read carefully: it deals with Gould's decision to back the plan for separation; he felt committed (p.378), for it was his only chance of keeping the mine. The author emphasises Gould's serious nature, even fanaticism, for by his ever deeper involvement in politics, he is sacrificing his wife's happiness. In this chapter we read also the description of Dr Monygham's torture. A significant and interesting character is thus added to the book, more than half way through; Conrad has carefully not revealed too many facts early.

NOTES AND GLOSSARY

lepero: (*Spanish*) lower class person

viva la libertad!: (*Spanish*) long live freedom!

practicante: (*Spanish*) trainee doctor

insidiously corrupted his judgment: gradually, without his noticing it, prevented him from thinking clearly

the cupidity of mankind: men's evil greed for possessions

flat acquiescence in illegality: complete acceptance of illegal acts

ransomed its way through all those years: it had bought peace and absence of interference, by bribery

a nauseous process: it made one sick to think about it

enlightened zeal: reforming enthusiasm (an ironical use of 'enlightened' since Conrad means the opposite, that is, he was completely reactionary)

quailed: trembled in fear

blind him indissolubly like a procedure of naturalization: prevented him from leaving the country as though he had lost his own nationality

Chapter 5

The arrival of Pedro (also called Pedrito) Montero was greeted by the Sulaco mob with great enthusiasm. As brother of the general who now controlled the capital and the rest of Costaguana, Pedro intended to make himself rich, but meanwhile he was disgusted to find that the interior of the Intendencia, the official residence of the Governor, had been very severely damaged by the town mob.

COMMENTARY: The arrival of Pedro Montero gives Conrad an opportunity to discuss the psychology of revolutionary leaders and the causes of revolution in general; he describes these (p.387) as 'the political immaturity of the people, the indolence of the upper classes and the mental darkness of the lower'.

NOTES AND GLOSSARY

lazo: (*Spanish*) lasso, rope thrown to catch horses etc.
gift of plausibility: ability to produce convincing arguments
largesse: money or gifts handed over generously
ciudadanos: (*Spanish*) citizens
plebiscite: vote of the whole nation on any given question, used often by authoritarian governments to obtain approval for their actions
étagère, console: (*French*) small table or set of shelves
his ingenuousness cherished this sign of his rank: like a child he was fond of this way of displaying his importance
mantas: (*Spanish*) blankets
pulperias: (*Spanish*) taverns
without parley: attacked without giving them a chance to surrender

Chapter 6

Don Pépé, who was in charge of the San Tomé mine, received a message from Montero asking him to surrender the mine. He discussed the situation with Father Roman, the resident priest. Don Pépé had received instructions from Charles Gould to blow up the mine and all its buildings rather than hand them over to any armed force, and he was prepared to do this.

COMMENTARY: Don Pépé is shown to be reliable as a defender of the mine.

NOTES AND GLOSSARY

haciendas: (*Spanish*) cattle sheds
alcalde: (*Spanish*) mayor
divine dispensation: what had been decided by Heaven
beside himself: losing control over himself

Chapter 7

Gould himself had been summoned to the Intendencia by Pedro Montero. He made it clear to Montero that any move to take over the mine would lead to its destruction, which would in turn bring a great loss to the country. Montero tried to remain friendly and even suggested that Gould might be given high rank by the new government with the title of Count or Marquis.

Meanwhile Dr Monygham decided that he could help by playing, as he said, 'a game of betrayal' with Sotillo, whom he would keep busy looking for the silver.

COMMENTARY: This chapter is a further reminder of Gould's fanaticism over the mine which is based on his ideal of justice. The author quotes the phrase 'Let the heavens fall' which is a translation from the Latin saying: Let the heavens fall, so long as justice is done: *'Fiat justitia ruat coelum'*.

NOTES AND GLOSSARY

effusion: expressing himself openly and warmly
grand seigneur: (*French*) great lord
the audience was over: the interview he had granted (as to an inferior subject)
without compunction: without regretting the consequences
tamper with him: interfere with his fidelity to his employers, probably by bribery or threats
loco: (*Spanish*) madman
his lair: where he had been lying hidden

Chapter 8

Nostromo had swum from the sinking lighter to the shore, choosing a hiding-place in the old fort by the harbour. There he had slept through the day. When he woke he felt even more strongly the feeling of resentment that had been recently creeping over him towards the rich Europeans who had used him for their own advantage and he was tempted to leave the country. But for the moment his footsteps turned in the direction of the Customs House where he met Dr Monygham who had come to find Sotillo. They discovered the body of Hirsch left behind after cruel torture. The doctor explained his plan to deceive and delay Sotillo by pretending to know where the treasure could be found. The doctor took Nostromo into his confidence because he hoped Nostromo would agree to go as messenger to Cayta to get Barrios to return to Sulaco with his troops.

COMMENTARY: The story switches back to Nostromo after an interval of several chapters. His difficulty in accepting his new situation is fully described; 'he remained rich in glory and reputation' (p.415) but his vanity could no longer be satisfied by any public appearance. His superstitious side is also emphasised. An even more significant aspect of his psychology now comes out clearly for the first time, though Decoud had begun to notice it earlier; this is Nostromo's sense that he has been exploited by his masters. As a result he no longer is loyal. The incorruptibility for which he was famous has disappeared. He allows the doctor to continue to believe that the treasure is lost. Dr Monygham's character is also further revealed (p.439); in his respectful love for Mrs Gould, he is ready to risk death. Nostromo now keeps to himself the reason for Hirsch's death at the hands of Sotillo.

NOTES AND GLOSSARY

it was not in keeping: his situation (as a man obliged to hide) did not fit in with his splendid reputation

a subjective nature: Nostromo had a character which made him think of everything that happened only in connection with himself; anything that hurt his vanity was a blow

Vecchio: (*Italian*) the old man

ya-acabo: (*Spanish*) already finished

sacrilegious guilt: he felt he had broken a sacred law (by not obeying the dying woman)

palmares: (*Spanish*) palm groves

evanescent quality: a quality that quickly disappears

given the estrapade: tortured by dropping from a height while attached to a rope

providential: (here) just at the right moment to help them

the very man: just the man who was wanted

intrepidity: bravery

mollified: his irritation was calmed

affected and curt nonchalance: he spoke briefly, pretending not to attach much importance to his own actions

unconsidered whim: unimportant idea that had come into their heads

a mere sham got up to deceive: just a pretence intended to trick

his heart steeled against remorse: his heart was hardened and he had no room to feel pity

in a spirit of abasement: purposely humiliating himself

Chapter 9

Sotillo had ordered the torture of Hirsch because he had made himself believe that the silver was not lost and that Hirsch must know where it was. Finally in anger he had killed Hirsch.

Monygham, as he talked to Nostromo, mentioned that he might give Sotillo the idea that the silver was hidden in the island of the Great Isabel. When Nostromo heard this, he had great difficulty in controlling his voice, but he persuaded the doctor instead that it would be better to suggest that the silver had been sunk in the harbour.

The doctor left Nostromo at the hotel where he found Viola silently mourning his wife's death. Viola gave Nostromo food and encouraged him to believe that he was still the man who could save them all, which had been the dying hope of his wife. Nostromo was deeply affected by this, as he felt guilt for not having fetched a priest for her when she was dying and he had been obliged to go on his mission with the silver.

COMMENTARY: As the doctor argues with Nostromo to persuade him to go to fetch General Barrios, we see the tension in Nostromo, whose mind is full of thoughts of the hidden silver. Nostromo only decides to undertake the mission after hearing that Viola's wife, before dying, had called upon him to save her children, who are in Mrs Gould's care. So we understand that Nostromo's superstitious sense of guilt was a strong motive in making him act subsequently as he did. This explanation of the inner workings of Nostromo's mind is of the utmost value in making the whole story credible.

NOTES AND GLOSSARY

muy valliente: (*Spanish*) very valiant, a title of flattery

ponchos: (*Spanish*) cloaks made of thick wool

jalousies: (*French*) blinds of the window

malediction!: curse! (not used in ordinary English; used here to recall the Spanish)

working himself up to the right pitch of ferocity: deliberately bringing himself into a state of sufficient anger (in order to frighten Hirsch)

sangre de Dios!: (*Spanish*) blood of God!

brazen: totally impudent, shameless

bribon: (*Spanish*) cheat

it was borne in on him: he suddenly began to realise

forfeited the right: lost, through his own fault, any right

siempre: (*Spanish*) always

the treasure . . . spirited away: removed secretly and rapidly

evil eye: the power of hurting another person by looking at them

Chapter 10

In later years, Captain Mitchell used to tell the story of those exciting days. He would show important visitors round the new city that had grown up, pointing out the main buildings and the places where there had been fighting and where Barrios's soldiers had re-entered the town. There were people also who had survived: Hernandez the bandit who had become Minister of War; Mrs Gould, the most respected lady in the land; Dr Monygham, who was now the National Inspector of Hospitals. Captain Mitchell would also tell how Nostromo had carried the vital message to Barrios in Cayta to request his return to Sulaco; Nostromo had gone four hundred miles through enemy-held territory, riding the first hundred in a locomotive along the newly built railway.

What Mitchell did not know was how Nostromo had discovered Decoud's dinghy—the boat that Decoud had kept with him on the island when he remained behind with the silver. There were marks of blood on the boat and, when Nostromo searched the hiding place of the silver, he found that four ingots (large bars) had disappeared. Thus Nostromo was the only person who knew that Decoud had met his end in an exceptional way, not by drowning in the lighter full of silver, as everybody supposed. He had committed suicide in solitude and despair. Nostromo now saw that, because he himself had put the silver before everything else, he had abandoned first Viola's wife as she lay dying and needed a priest, and then Decoud, who had been left to die. These deaths would now always remain on the conscience of Nostromo and this was the price he had begun to pay for possession of the silver treasure. It only made him all the more determined to make no mistakes; so as to avoid discovery, his first decision was 'I must grow rich very slowly.'

COMMENTARY: Although still far from the end of the novel, the author gives us, through Mitchell, a view into the future. We learn of Sulaco's prosperity after the war. We also see the way Nostromo discovered how Decoud had committed suicide; this was a further burden on his conscience from then onwards. Strangely, though, it only increases his determination to make no mistake over the treasure—'I must grow rich very slowly.'

NOTES AND GLOSSARY

man-about-town: a man who is constantly seen in the best society

burros: (*Spanish*) donkeys

a fair likeness: quite a good resemblance

taken the veil: become a nun, go into a convent

camorra: (*Italian*) Italian secret society

snarly: with a snarl or unpleasant smile

big-wig: important person

begad: (an old-fashioned expletive) by God!

I could spin you a yarn: tell you a story

as cool as you please: quite without any shame

cadging for smokes: asking people to give him cigars (or cigarettes)
taking a rise out of him: making him a fool without his realising it
become a second nature: grown quite natural
guffaw: to laugh loudly and stupidly
cielo!: (*Spanish*) heaven!
nothing short of main force: only if he had been held back by force could he have been stopped

Chapter 11

Mr and Mrs Gould returned to Costaguana after a second prolonged visit to Europe. A number of years had passed since the troubles in Sulaco. Dr Monygham, whose devotion to Mrs Gould had not altered or decreased, was having a discussion with her about Antonia Avellanos and her uncle, now Cardinal-Archbishop of Sulaco. The doctor remarked that they were incorrigible (they could never be reformed; they would always be like this) political plotters and that they had the support of the secret societies amongst whom Nostromo was an acknowledged leader. Nostromo's power with the people was greater than ever before. The doctor had noticed the fact that now the workers at the Gould mine were no longer grateful or friendly to their Señor Administrador or manager, Charles Gould.

The doctor had an interesting piece of gossip to report about Nostromo. He was regularly courting Linda, the elder daughter of his old Italian friend Viola. On his return from a voyage, Nostromo, who was reported to be making his fortune by trading, found that a lighthouse was being built on the island of the Great Isabel. Nostromo had then proposed his friend and he had been appointed as lighthouse keeper.

One of old Viola's reasons for accepting the job had been that it made it easier to take his younger daughter Giselle away from the attentions of a man of whom he disapproved. But Dr Monygham said that this man, Ramirez, who was much in love, complained not just that Viola was against him but that Nostromo himself was interested in the younger girl as much as in Linda to whom he was officially engaged.

The doctor took his leave and Mrs Gould remained alone to meditate on what he had said, particularly about the 'incorrigible' nature of people. She thought about her husband who had devoted his life and energy to the mine; he had been immensely successful, but his love for her had been swallowed up by his material preoccupations; and she thought of another sad fact—everything had been sacrificed for a great achievement but they had no children to whom they could pass on the inheritance; they would be the last of the Costaguana Goulds.

COMMENTARY: The end of this chapter returns to the theme of Charles Gould's obsession with the mine, that brings sadness to Mrs Gould. The phrases 'moral degradation' and 'material interest' sum up her attitude, but there is nothing she can do. (The question of 'material interest' is taken up again in Part III, chapter 11, p.509 & p.511.)

NOTES AND GLOSSARY

tertulia: (*Spanish*) party or reception

lovelorn swain: (an old phrase, used ironically) unhappy lover

Chapter 12

Nostromo's nature had been subtly changed by the secret of the treasure; he had lost his peace of mind. And he had discovered that he preferred Giselle, the younger sister, to his fiancée Linda. He had been led to suggest Viola for the job of lighthouse-keeper so as to have an excuse for visiting the island when secretly he went to take silver from his treasure. Nostromo had gone one day to ask Viola to give him his younger daughter in marriage but Viola had misunderstood him and had brought forward Linda who had never hidden her love for the great Nostromo. At this terrible moment of misunderstanding Nostromo had been afraid to insist on his true preference, for fear that Viola might then forbid him to visit the island, which would mean he could not get to the treasure.

But it meant that Nostromo had had a passionate love-affair with Giselle while pretending to court Linda. Giselle had implored him to take her away but he went so far as to tell her that he had a secret treasure which kept him in Sulaco.

COMMENTARY: The strange story of Nostromo's love affair with the younger Viola sister is told rapidly. We get the impression that Nostromo is now a man who has lost control over his life, even though he has shown the greatest prudence in using the treasure.

NOTES AND GLOSSARY

a chip off the old block: resembling one's parent

he allowed it to get about: he started the rumour

Lodge: meeting of the secret society

his knowledge . . . had not played him false: what he had remembered (about Viola's character) had proved perfectly true

Misericordia Divina!: (*Italian*) Mercy of God!

Santissima Madre!: (*Italian*) Most Holy Mother!

frittura: (*Italian*) fried dish

Chapter 13

Viola's suspicions of Ramirez increased, for he had heard rumours that he was coming to the island to carry Giselle away. He knew nothing about Nostromo's hidden love. Linda suffered terribly, but resolved to say nothing. Viola got into the habit of walking at night about the island, which was otherwise uninhabited, with a loaded gun. One night he shot Nostromo who was visiting his treasure, thinking that Nostromo was Ramirez. Nostromo was carried, dying, to the hospital in Sulaco where he asked to see Mrs Gould.

He offered to tell Mrs Gould the secret of the treasure but she refused to hear. She took Giselle home with her. Mrs Gould felt a connection with this girl who had lost her lover, because they both loved men who had given their hearts to silver and its strange power.

Giorgio Viola did not survive the shock when Linda told him that, instead of killing Ramirez as he thought, he had killed his old friend Nostromo whom he had long hoped to make his son-in-law. Linda, alone in the lighthouse, swore she would never forget Nostromo, convinced that her sister on the other hand, although she had gained his love, was incapable of such loyalty. So ends Conrad's story of 'the magnificent figure of the Capataz de Cargadores' and the dark, mysterious gulf of Sulaco 'containing his conquests of treasure and love.'

COMMENTARY: Like the previous chapter, this moves forward with dramatic speed and it gains strength from its simple telling. There is a tragic nobility about his end that suits Nostromo's character. We seem to hear Conrad saying: 'Here at least was a real man.'

NOTES AND GLOSSARY

his faculties unimpaired: his mind was as alert as ever

gratuitous outrage: the unnecessary, additional insult

drove her beside herself: maddened her

pull easy: row gently (a naval term)

stern sheets: back corner of boat (a nautical expression)

Part 3

Commentary

The nature of the work

Nostromo is a full-length novel, written at the very beginning of the twentieth century (1903–4). It is written in a style and with a form that largely follow the English tradition of the novel as it had been developed to that date. Nevertheless, the reader who is familiar with other works by Conrad will easily see that there is much in the way of writing that is typical of Conrad and which can be called his own individual contribution to the growth of the English novel. Conrad was strongly influenced, as was mentioned in Part 1, by the tradition of the long short story, a form of fiction more usual on the Continent than in England, and it may be said that this was the form that suited him best, and which enabled him to produce his artistically most successful works. *Nostromo*, with all its detail and its length, put a great strain on the author's powers of control and organisation of subject-matter, and in places the interest of the story is slightly lost. But without any doubt Conrad produced a work that is of the first rank, belonging to the nineteenth century rather than the twentieth—for it is not experimental—but highly individual, so that every page seems to have his personal signature. It will be necessary to consider subsequently, then, what the general tradition of the nineteenth century novel involved and what Conrad's own contribution to it was.

The purpose of the work

Nostromo was clearly produced (like many great works of art) with the immediate intention by the author of making money. Its first purpose therefore is to entertain readers by providing a story which will hold and grip their attention. By choosing subjects that were much in the public's mind at that time (Latin-American revolutions and fortune-making through silver and gold) Conrad made sure that his contemporary readers would come to his book with ready interest—though this applies slightly less today, some seventy years later.

In this type of novel the aim is to concentrate the reader's attention mainly on one hero, in this case Nostromo, and on some significant period of his life, in this case the last half, from his arrival in Sulaco till his death. This concentration on the affairs of one main character does not, however, prevent the author from also giving us a rich background of other personalities who may provide a parallel (for example, Charles Gould) or a contrast (such as Corbelán). In addition Conrad drew a picture of a strange world of adventure and drama that would satisfy the average English reader's taste for the excitement which did not easily come his way in the quiet England that he knew. We must remember that at this time England had been free from any major war for a period of ninety years, since the final defeat of Napoleon in 1815. Unlike most other countries in Western Europe, England had not suffered from any revolutions at all in the course of the nineteenth century. Thus the stable conditions of the time made English readers particularly interested in following the story of a world so different, and Conrad, who had personally experienced the tragedy of revolution in his own country, was well equipped to deal with this subject.

The achievement of the work

Conrad's achievement in *Nostromo* must be counted as something more than the writing of a long novel of adventure. His real achievement lies in the artistic quality of its form. By the word 'form' we mean the control that an artist in any art exercises over the material. Whatever the art—literature, painting, music or any other—it is essential that details should not get out of control and that every part of the work should contribute towards the total effect. This is true of *Nostromo*. If we analyse the book carefully, we shall see that Conrad has aimed to put in nothing that does not help us to feel what he wants us to feel. His message is not so easy to sum up in a few words, but perhaps the main thing is the strangeness of life of which he gives us an example in the story of a man whose ups and downs make us realize that the future can never be safely predicted. Furthermore, good comes out of bad and bad out of good, so that success may really mean failure. Life is infinitely complicated and is certainly not just what it seems. This message lies behind the story of outward adventure and it is Conrad's achievement that, when we put down the book, we have a sense that we have learned something about the mystery of life, and this counts for more than just having read an unusual story.

Social and historical background

We must consider the background of the novel from two points of view; first, what had been happening in South America and what it meant to Conrad and his readers; second, what sort of England was the book published in, and how far did it resemble or differ from the England of today?

South America, in the course of the nineteenth century, had been the scene of ceaseless struggles for power, involving, to begin with, many separate small wars to secure independence from the Spanish and Portuguese masters. Once independent republics had been formed, however, there was a renewal in many places of military activity and civil disorder as new governments and dictators arose with new revolutionary ideals or personal ambitions. This meant that the heroic days of fighting in the noble, common cause of independence were succeeded by a period when many men questioned the ability and honesty of their leaders, who in turn fought to retain the power which they had torn from others.

This was the general picture in everybody's minds at the turn of the century and Conrad knew that by setting his story against such a background he could expect his readers to understand more or less the atmosphere of mingled cynicism and idealism which he describes. He refers at one point (Part I, Chapter 6) to Bolivar, the great hero of the wars of independence, whose integrity had been beyond dispute. Both a general and a man of politics, Bolivar had come close to uniting several of the newly formed independent republics in one federation. But he had failed in his efforts and Conrad's imaginary dictator, Guzman Bento, was typical of the sort of man whose later brutal seizure of power had left the idealist politician Don José Avellanos (also, of course, an imaginary portrait) in a position of helpless opposition.

Garibaldi, leader in the Italian wars of national independence, had also for many years fought at the head of a small, heroic force of international volunteers, operating both on sea and land along the coasts of South America. Nostromo's friend, Giorgio Viola, whose past as a 'Garibaldino' (or follower of Garibaldi, see note on p.13) was well-known, is another representative, apart from Don José, of the idealistic side of politics that was so totally contrasted to the authoritarian powers they fought, both in ideals and methods. Conrad regards these men with admiration and pity. They were ineffective and seemed lost in a new and more violent age that often considered them unrealistic.

In the same way we see that Conrad refers more than once to the connection between the early heroic idealism and Britain. Viola is shown to remember his own leader's special devotion to the English, for Garibaldi had been received as a hero by the English people when he came to England, while British governments had on several occasions given him decisive support in Italy. Another even more direct connection with the British was to be found in their policy, firmly established by Canning, when Foreign Secretary in the 1820s, of supporting the struggle for independence at all points on the South American continent. Thus the Gould family, in Conrad's novel, could feel that their presence in Costaguana was no accident but was the result of an historical process of interaction between two freedom-loving communities. They were there for trade, but in their opinion they were also there to represent a noble tradition. Conrad never hid his admiration for England, his adopted country, and he is careful to show, in this story, that Charles Gould was not a man to be judged too severely. For Gould devoted his life to his mine, not just for money but in order to compensate for his father's failure, and when he had a chance to influence politics directly, he chose to support progressive governments.

The subject of fortune-making through mining is really separate from South American history, but Conrad united the two themes in this book. In the latter half of the nineteenth century people had often woken to the news that a new 'Gold Rush' or 'Diamond Rush' had begun. The opening-up of the vast unexplored territories of South Africa, Australia and America (especially Alaska) had brought many sudden discoveries of extraordinarily rich deposits of minerals. Adventurers of all sorts rushed to the spot, and fortunes were often made—and sometimes also lost—in a few weeks. The Sulaco silver mine that Conrad imagined was not such a sudden discovery, for its site had long been known. However, it was thought to lie under a curse and its successful exploitation under Charles Gould only came after many unsuccessful attempts had been made. But Conrad describes a process that was very typical of his period when he shows that the decisive moment arrives when Gould is able to obtain large-scale financial backing from a United States millionaire who was interested in his project. This was very much the age of the financier; people were becoming aware that industry and even politics, to be successful, must have adequate financial support. The British Prime Minister Disraeli had been able to buy a controlling share in the Suez Canal only through the aid of the international bankers, the Rothschilds; while it was common knowledge that in the United States itself, financiers such as Commodore Vanderbilt (1796–1877) and John Pierpont Morgan (1837–1913) had power that was like that of the kings and emperors.

The social background in Britain

Conrad wrote *Nostromo* at a time when other writers were concentrating on urgent social problems at home in Britain and it could be said that, in comparison with their works, his novel is 'escapist' literature, intended to attract the attention of people who preferred not to think about what it was really a citizen's duty to think about. Shaw and Galsworthy*

*George Bernard Shaw (1856–1950), an Irish author, wrote many very successful plays which put forward controversial ideas in lively form. Socialism influenced his thought but his attitude in politics was independent and questioning. John Galsworthy (1867-1933) was a novelist and playwright, famous for his trilogy *The Forsyte Saga*.

were reminding theatre-audiences that injustice and ill-treatment of the poor were only too frequent in their own country; Wells* was describing the hardships of the lower middle class; Bennett† showed the nation what struggles took place in an industrial society. In contrast to such writers Conrad seemed always to turn his eyes away from the ordinary man's immediate concern.

The nation was in a serious mood of self-criticism, following on a long period of self-congratulation in the reign of Queen Victoria. The Queen's death in 1901 brought a whole era to a close, for she had reigned for over sixty years, during which time the country had changed immeasurably and had moved into modern times. The Victorians had shown immense energy, the country had been covered by railways and roads, an extraordinary number of factories and buildings of all sorts had been put up, numerous new towns created and the wealth of the nation increased by trade and every form of industrial activity. But in the process of getting rich, somehow the nation had made many men poor and, what is worse, unhappy. Slum conditions had developed which were a disgrace to civilisation: workers in the heart of London were being exploited in ways that would hardly have been possible in distant colonies.

But this was not the side of life that interested Conrad. In the first place he was a foreigner by birth who had not settled down in England till his late thirties; he did not have much opportunity to get to know closely the social circumstances of the majority of the population; he lived for his writing, which now occupied all his time, and he lived in a part of the country—the south east—where conditions were the most satisfactory in many ways and social discontent was rare. In any case, he was a man of the sea, a traveller, an adventurer by nature; in the twenty years or so since he had begun writing, the subjects that had suggested themselves to him for stories had all come from his wide personal experience of distant parts of the world and the English-reading public had turned with interest to such stories. It was not unnatural that Conrad should have tried in *Nostromo* to create another plot, this time dealing with a part of the world of which he had no first-hand knowledge but similar in some ways to countries he knew.

Finally, it may be said that Conrad was dealing with a subject which he knew about, conditions under a revolution. This was also a subject on which he felt strongly.

*Herbert George Wells (1866–1946), a scientific writer and novelist, was also a convinced Socialist. A man of humble origins, he treated social themes humanely and gained widespread popularity.

†Arnold Bennett (1867–1931) was a journalist and realistic novelist who established his reputation with his *Old Wives' Tale* (1908), a novel about the industrial north of England.

The structure

Conrad's novel is carefully constructed, as we can see by examining the way the story unfolds. We notice the various devices that the author uses to maintain the interest of the reader and it is clear that Conrad, conscious perhaps that the book is a long one, pays great attention to the need to vary his method of presentation. Without going into questions of style—which will be examined in the next section—we may say that the novel is constructed mainly round the activities of the hero Nostromo, and the story is mainly told by the author himself, who writes as though he were in possession of all the necessary information, however secret or private the facts. This way of writing can be described as that of the 'omniscient author'; in other words Conrad speaks as if, by some magic means, he knew everything—even what was in the hearts and minds of his characters, perhaps even thoughts and feelings that they would never have revealed to anyone else, or hardly even made clear to themselves. A good example of this would be what Conrad says about Dr Monygham's shame at his inability in the past to stand up to torture; another example might be Nostromo's decision to continue concealing the treasure.

This method of writing has great advantages and has been used by the majority of novelists. It allows the story to be told simply without worrying the reader with too many accounts given by supposed witnesses, for it is surprising how little any one person can know of a chain of events such as those described in a novel. We notice this when Conrad, for the sake of variation, gives us parts of the story as seen through the eyes of Captain Mitchell or Martin Decoud (when he writes his extremely long letter to his sister). What these two characters describe reveals only part of the truth; this is obvious when we find that Mitchell's ideas about the past and present of Sulaco are over-simple and are ridiculed by the author shortly afterwards.

As the 'omniscient author' is telling the story, he is able to write at his leisure and go into as much detail as he likes. So we find that he gives us an introductory description in the first chapter of the geography and history of Sulaco, which tells us all about the frightening, sinister reputation of the silver mine and prepares us for the whole story of its bad influence. Only an author who is concerned to construct his novel carefully would have gone into such detail. Another example of conscious construction can be taken from the end of the book. The symbolic cloud of silver, together with the dramatic cry of Linda Viola, have been chosen as a suitable ending, but they do not add much to the story and are hardly necessary.

Another point to notice is that Conrad makes much use of the 'flashback'—a trick often employed in the cinema as well as in novels, so that the story moves backward for a while, sometimes through the memory of one of the characters as in the case of Mitchell. The disadvantage of the 'flashback' device is that it may leave the reader confused, even though the past has become vivid.

There is an outward division of the book into three parts which correspond more or less to the action of the story as far as it concerns Nostromo. But because Conrad thought it necessary to tell us many things apart from the story of Nostromo himself, these three parts are not completely logical and we may wonder whether their main use is not simply to divide up a book that would otherwise appear overlong.

The style

Style, being the general manner or habit of writing of any given author, is something that may remain very much the same in all his different works, varying only with his developing experience and the nature of the work itself. *Nostromo* belongs to what may be called the middle period of Conrad's writing career and shows his powers to the full. The style is the mature style of a writer who has learnt how to control his material, even though complicated, and how to present his characters, even though there are several quite detailed portraits.

In Part 1 we discussed the influence that the English language itself had on Conrad's way of writing. It was for him a foreign language painfully acquired by hard study, but full of astonishing rewards. It gave him not just the means of reaching and pleasing a large section of the world's public but also an extraordinary richness of phrase of which he was quick to take advantage. The result is that Conrad's books, including *Nostromo*, are sometimes more full of striking expressions and colloquial or technical language than novels by native English writers. A noticeable example of this is his frequent inclusion of sailing terms which appear whenever boats or the sea are mentioned—for instance, Dr Monygham (on the last page) stands 'in the stern sheets' of the boat. Again, when the conversation of his characters is reported, Conrad always enjoys putting into their mouths language that is typically spoken rather than written. Sometimes he even overdoes this when we feel that he is almost saying: 'Look what a remarkable command I have of the English language, even of slang!' So we find Captain Mitchell says at one point: 'Begad, sir! I could spin you a yarn for hours . . .' and, a little later, 'He stopped me as cool as you please, with a request for a cigar . . . it's a confounded nuisance. The fellow's everlastingly cadging for smokes.' The disadvantage of slang is that it goes out of date and then makes the conversation sound old-fashioned, even silly.

However, anyone comparing Conrad's novels with those of lesser writers must be struck by the unusual quality of his language that can best be expressed by the word 'poetic'. (For further discussion of this point, see the model essay in Part 4 on 'Conrad as a poet among novelists'.) His choice of image to illustrate his meaning is nearly always striking and powerful; for example, he says of Viola after his wife's death: 'His soul had descended into the open abyss of desolation amongst the shattered vestiges of his past.' And he describes Charles Gould, ready if necessary to destroy the mine rather than surrender it to the revolutionaries, as having 'something of the spirit of a buccaneer throwing a lighted match into the magazine rather than surrender his ship.'

But perhaps the most impressive single characteristic of Conrad's style is his use of irony. Irony is a method of criticism which avoids direct speaking; very often the exact reverse is said of what the writer really means. Even if it is not quite the opposite, the writer shows that he is not serious. Somehow this indirect method seemed to suit Conrad, who resembled in so many ways the English he admired. For it is an English characteristic to prefer to avoid direct or violent attack, believing that a criticism that is made quietly is often more effective. This is similar to the fondness for 'understatement', which, as everyone knows, can be just as striking as exaggeration. It is natural therefore to expect to find irony whenever Conrad is describing a character or situation which he dislikes, and it is above all in such passages that we should look for examples.

The characters

Nostromo

Although the book bears his name as its title, Nostromo does not entirely dominate the novel. There are in reality two parallel plots, one of which is concerned with the growth of the mine under Charles Gould. What Nostromo does has relatively little effect on this side of the story, for his concealment of one consignment of silver is relatively insignificant compared with the vast political and economic development that the Gould concession represents. Only one action of Nostromo's is of significance on this larger scale, and that is his dash through the enemy-held territory to fetch General Barrios and his troops back to Sulaco. We may imagine that what he did earlier to fight the mob was useful work but did not vitally alter the situation.

As a result, although Nostromo is introduced in the first part of the novel, indeed even in the very first pages, we do not feel that his character properly emerges until later—and it is then that we see its dark side. At the beginning we only know him through his public reputation, particularly as spread by his employer, Captain Mitchell, who is so proud of having discovered him and is so satisfied with his work. We learn that he is energetic and efficient, a born leader of men and ready to fight as well as to organise. We are not told anything about his past, however, and when we come to analyse the beginning of the book closely, we see that we at first get to know more about his abilities than about his inner character. Efficiency and leadership do not tell us much about a man's secret sources of energy or deep motivations.

There is, however, one point that Conrad offers as a clue to the interpretation of Nostromo's character, and that is his vanity. He is proud, not just of his appearance, but also of his reputation. Probably he works especially well for Captain Mitchell because his employer shows openly how highly he thinks of him. It is this same weakness of vanity that leads gradually to Nostromo's crime. For he is not a man who acts according to true conscience, but only for superficial reasons, in order to appear in a good light. Even his little acts of generosity, such as his present of silver buttons to his young lover, come from a desire to appear generous rather than from true love. He does not seem to have deep emotions, or at least none which in any way bind him to other people.

So when the idea begins to grow in his mind that he is being exploited by the powerful and the rich in Sulaco, he ceases to have any impulse of true loyalty towards his employers who, he now believes, are using his services without adequately rewarding him. The development of this new attitude of mind is very well shown by Conrad. It is a subtle change, and gradual. Thus we are not surprised at all when we find that he gives in to the temptation to let everyone believe that the silver treasure has been lost. From this point it is only natural that his life should be organised round his own need to collect the treasure from its hiding-place and, as he promised to himself, 'get rich gradually'. Significantly, however, Conrad says that Nostromo felt that something had gone out of his life, which was his pleasure in leading his life in the public eye and receiving constant public approval; this he could no longer do. Thus it was not his conscience that hurt him; but his vanity was no longer satisfied. His activities in Sulaco now centred on secret societies and, of course, on his hidden treasure.

Finally, we have the strange story of his secret passion for Giselle Viola and his affair with her that goes on while he remains officially engaged to be married to her elder sister. Conrad could not have imagined a more appropriate end; it seems right and proper that this man whose life has moved into dark ways should be shot at night and by a mistake. Such a death comes as a fitting climax to a career both mysterious and unusual.

Charles Gould

Charles Gould is interesting for his own sake and also as a contrast or parallel to Nostromo. His character is portrayed clearly and sympathetically from the beginning. He is a man with a mission, somebody who feels compelled to act as he does, not primarily for material gain or even worldly power, but rather in order to face a challenge that confronts him. He feels that his task in life is to carry out work which his father was unable to manage. As he has dedicated himself to this task, he overlooks the fact that he is directly disobeying the instructions of his father, constantly repeated, that he should turn away from the mine. He feels that it is right that he should take no notice of what his father said, precisely because he should not act out of fear or cowardice; in other words, he rejects his father's advice as being negative; he himself is determined to be positive.

His relations with his wife are typical of a character of this kind, strong and single-minded. He is truly fond of her and relies implicitly on her support, but Conrad shows very well how he comes more and more to take this support as a matter of course. He ceases to respond fully to her feminine demand for love. Conrad also seems to wish to show that this demand for love does not represent a selfish instinct, but is founded on a sense of reality that she is right to follow, as opposed to her husband's dedication to material interests.

For this is what has happened to Charles Gould. His life in a sense, has changed into the opposite of what he had intended it to be. He is shown as someone who, from youth upwards has been idealistic, wishing to help mankind, and he is not reactionary in his political attitude. He has inherited the reputation and way of thinking of his uncle, who was so cruelly treated and killed by the previous tyrannical government. But Charles consciously makes the decision to compromise whenever necessary for the sake of achieving his main aim—the development of the mine. As a result, his heart hardens in a subtle way. His wife exclaims: 'Material interests' (end of Part II, Chapter 6) but this is not the whole trouble. There is also the curse of the mine, a theme which lies behind the whole book and which links the destiny of Charles Gould with Nostromo's. Both men have their lives ruined in the end by the silver, though in very different ways.

Other smaller touches need to be noticed, apart from the main drama of Charles's life. He is described as very English in several ways—in his appearance, for Conrad gives him bright red hair and makes him a great horse-rider. He is also shown as practical, determined and courageous—a man who rises superior to all the small intrigues and obstacles by which he is surrounded. He is independent-minded; conscious of the power of his money, but also unafraid of giving offence to people he despises, he does not trouble to hide his arrogance from the local men of influence whom he bribes (Part II, Chapter 7).

Finally, we must not forget that he is a man with two countries, but he reconciles his divided loyalties by his strong positive desire to use his English strength of character to promote the welfare of the country where he lives. It is not entirely his fault if circumstances gradually spoil the purity of his aim.

Mrs Gould

Mrs Gould is one of the characters who are drawn entirely sympathetically. She is an integral part of the novel, not so much for her influence on the action, which is indirect, as for her moral significance. She redresses the balance of good against evil. Conrad knew by instinct that if he concentrated too exclusively on depicting the bad effects of the search for money and power he would tire the reader and would cease to be convincing. By introducing a truly good person like Mrs Gould, Conrad is able to contrast black with white, and also—a useful technical point for a novelist—to provide a character who is in some ways detached from the others and who can act as an observer. What Mrs Gould says to herself about 'Material interests' when she sadly reflects that her husband is no longer so close to her, can be seen also as part of Conrad's own message in the novel.

It is always extremely difficult for a writer to draw a good person, because goodness is not self-assertive and therefore often seems uninteresting. Perhaps the feminine qualities that Mrs Gould possesses offer Conrad the best chance to show this goodness. She truly loves her husband for his own sake and not for anything he can bring her. Rather, she loves him in spite of what he brings her—which is a sense of inner failure. She realised the emptiness of material success, and she also deeply regrets that she has been unable to show Charles how to disengage himself from the struggle that has involved him too completely. The process by which Charles finds himself more and more obliged to compromise is very well described. When he was at school he took little notice of his father's warnings about the mine, because he was a realist and thought his father was getting excited about nothing. When he inherited the property, which was also the time of his marriage, he is shown under the impulse of strong enthusiasm—always an attractive quality in Conrad's eyes. Later, his courageous persistence in the face of endless difficulties also reveals a fine side of his nature. But gradually a point is reached when his activity has become an obsession that brings a drying-up of his nature. What was good has become bad. To show an inner change of this kind in a character is the mark of a fine novelist, for it is no easy task. A comparison with Captain Mitchell will show the the difference between a static and an evolving character.

The presence of Mrs Gould is necessary in order to provide a human picture of her husband. Otherwise we should easily come to think of him as a monster of efficiency, a man without any soul, who has given himself to the devil of the silver. In a way this is what he has done, but he has a fine human nature that has been spoiled by concentration on too narrow an aim. A very significant fact is the Goulds' childlessness. We feel that Mrs Gould regretted this not just because she had not provided her husband with an heir to continue the family line, but also because children would have meant that her husband had a strong interest and attachment to draw him away from the mine.

Dr Monygham

Dr Monygham should not be underestimated as a character. He plays a valuable part in the plot when he decides on his own initiative to delay Sotillo's entry into Sulaco by deceiving him with false stories about the silver, and this action marks a step in his inner progress towards regaining self-respect, for he voluntarily faces once more the danger of torture and death if his trick is discovered by Sotillo, as it may well be. But there is something more significant about him; he not only helps materially but he helps to rectify the spiritual balance of the situation. If we look carefully, we shall see that Conrad describes him as a man who acts from love and not from material interest. Typically and subtly, Conrad shows the paradox of his character; he is oversensitive, and precisely for this reason he is obliged to hide his feelings under a mask of bitterness and cynicism. As a result, he is often misjudged. Cleverly, Conrad allows the reader to misjudge him at first, for we see him only in a rather negative light and his only quality seems to be his devotion to Mrs Gould. Gradually Conrad reveals certains facts about his past, particularly his suffering under torture, which allow us to see that we are dealing with one of those complicated, unhappy personalities that teach us that appearances are often misleading.

For this reason Dr Monygham can be considered one of the most interesting characters in the book, psychologically speaking. And his association with Mrs Gould is no chance matter, because Conrad brings together two people whose actions are not motivated by 'material interests'; in the shadow of the curse of the silver, the purity of Dr Monygham's devotion to Mrs Gould is carefully emphasised; he wishes her truly well and this means that he includes her husband in his affection. There is no hint of possessiveness in his love for her, but there is much protectiveness. In addition we see him extending his desire to serve to a wide circle of people who do not always appreciate his kindness, for they have been deceived by his sarcastic manner. We may say that in him Conrad has given us a portrait in depth which contrasts with others, such as of Captain Mitchell, which, however interesting, are less subtle.

Captain Mitchell

Captain Mitchell is not a character who plays any active part in the story, except to take Nostromo into employment. The incident of his arrest by the soldiers of Sotillo has no real significance. Mitchell is nevertheless of importance, for he is the narrator to whom Conrad has given the responsibility of communicating a number of essential facts to the reader. In his book Conrad frequently uses the trick of speaking through somebody who is supposed to have been an original witness, and we can see that there are advantages in this, for as long as we believe in this witness, the story becomes more vivid and personal. Captain Mitchell is very well described at the beginning of the book; he is above all honest, and that is the very first quality needed in a narrator. Conrad also tells us that he is a little simple or naive, so this means that we can believe everything he says, but that his interpretation may not be quite the same as the author's. This adds an invaluable extra dimension to the story; an example is at the end, when Mitchell describes what has happened in Sulaco since the revolution. We can see that things are not so perfect as he thinks. (Here, as elsewhere, we can see the connection between Conrad's use of irony and his desire to put a certain distance between himself and the reader).

There are various other characteristics of Mitchell that are stressed, apart from his innocent honesty; he is slightly pompous and pleased with himself, but he is not aggressively so. Notice his behaviour at the time of his arrest: he is courageous even if flustered. He is kind and well-meaning, although he is not particularly intelligent. He is the type of reliable worker who rises to the top in his own little sphere, through his steady application and quiet confidence in his own abilities. Like Gould he seems to be an essentially English sort of person, as seen through the Polish eyes of Conrad. Probably an English writer would have had more to criticise in such a character, but for Conrad he represents on the whole an attractive person with valuable positive qualities.

Don José Avellanos

Don José Avellanos is shown by Conrad in an entirely favourable light, though his end is sad and full of disappointment. He is an idealist, of a generous temperament; he has given himself without reserve to the cause of progressive government and he has suffered much, in body as well as in mind. Together with Mrs Gould and Dr Monygham he completes the balance of the novel, which, without these three, would be over-concentrated on the negative sides of life. Conrad has few illusions about human nature, but he is not fundamentally a pessimist and does not, in this novel at least, intend to leave the reader with the feeling that struggle with evil is useless.

Don José is the type of man who can be called a statesman, as opposed to a mere politician. His aim is not personal advancement and he always bears in mind the good of the state. He is totally dedicated to politics, which have decided the course of his life, but he is not a fanatic, for he has nothing of the extremist about him. On the contrary. The lack of violence in his nature has left him in a middle position in politics that has brought him little active support, though over the years he has won wide respect. Conrad stresses this weakness in connection also with President Ribiera who is too trusting (as is shown in his choice of appointments) and unable to meet violence with violence. Here the realist in Conrad condemns a middle-of-the-road course, but we feel at the same time that he himself would not have been long in favour of any authoritarian government. This is the permanent problem of compromise, which is both unsatisfactory and yet necessary.

Don José's work is not useless, even though he believes that his life's work has been ruined by the revolution of the Montero brothers. He cannot know that he will leave behind some progress. He has guided his nation out of a very barbaric, primitive stage in politics and this achievement will not be wasted. On the other hand, Conrad is very doubtful whether there is much good in many aspects of so-called progress; he allows Captain Mitchell to talk complacently about the material development of Sulaco, its prosperity and power, but he makes it quite clear that these represent in fact superficial values. In any case Don José had been concerned with something deeper and, like Giorgio Viola, he had been a fighter in a more heroic age.

Martin Decoud

Martin Decoud is one of those characters whom Conrad treats with irony and almost a certain contempt. He is an adventurer, but not quite the type of brave and vigorous adventurer of whom Conrad is fond. He is rather a man who is too clever, living from day to day without any settled plan, for he really lacks strength of character to back up any decision he may take. As a journalist he manages to give the impression of being more able than he is; he has charm and intelligence, as we can see from the way he talks to Antonia and to Mrs Gould, both of whom know how to appreciate these sides of a man. We notice that it is he who revives the idea of separating Sulaco from the rest of Costaguana;

it is an idea for the future that is highly successful, though it does not easily convince Charles Gould or Don José. Thus Decoud is here quite practical, even though he seems to be playing with something rather unrealistic. However, he does not have the power to carry out his ideas, as is shown by his death, which comes through his own weakness of character. He is unable to support the solitude of the island; after a very few days he seeks a solution that can only be excused by his sleeplessness. Conrad seems to stress this lack of sleep as a physical symptom so that we feel pity for Decoud as a man who is suffering, but there is no respect for him as for Nostromo who meets his death with dignity and calm. Decoud's relations with Antonia also seem to be the result of a certain lack of control on his part, and we wonder how deeply she is in love with him. His attitude in love perhaps confirms what we feel in general about him, that he is a weakling, morally speaking.

Giorgio Viola

Giorgio Viola is one of those characters for whom Conrad obviously has an affection; he is the kind of man who adds something to life by his enthusiasm and devotion to an ideal. He may be a comparatively ignorant and unsophisticated person, but he is a real man, Conrad seems to say. For the same reason that Conrad admired his fellow-sailors, he approved of men who devoted themselves to some cause bigger tham themselves—they are men of action in the best sense, not aimlessly busy, but ready at all times to show their willingness to sacrifice themselves through deeds, not just words. The international activity of Garibaldi and his connection with England have already been commented on (see p.45). Conrad felt at home with such men, for he himself had chosen occupations—writing and life at sea—which were not chosen for gain. However, he does not identify himself fully with all selfless enthusiasts—in fact, at several points he shows that Viola is naive and belongs to a past that can no longer offer a realistic message. Viola inspires respect and interest in his fellow-countrymen, who gather nightly to hear his stories of heroism, but those who hear him lead very different lives and they are not even called to copy his example, for circumstances have changed. As for the local population, Viola's attitude towards them is more or less one of contempt, for they are so far from any ability to live on an heroic plane. This reminds us that in such a philosophy of life there is no room for practicality—it is a philosophy for an élite who tend to have an unreasoning belief in action for its own sake. When conditions are prosperous or stable, as occurs from time to time, their wings fall to the ground and they have little to offer—or alternatively, as in Nostromo's case, they go to the bad. The energy in them is used up in the wrong way and they become criminals or villains instead of heroes.

Part 4

Hints for study

How to analyse the novel

For the purpose of preparing for an examination, and also, in general, in order to appreciate any literary work, it is helpful to learn how to analyse the novel. We may enjoy reading the story or perhaps even we may find it hard to enjoy, but what we want to discover is its real merit, independent of our personal taste. Often we find, after looking at the different aspects of a book in this way, that our original impression is deepened and we are able to get more pleasure and interest out of it. The first point to consider is the external framework, by which is meant the incidents and the development of the story: this can be summed up by the word Plot. Secondly, we can try to decide how far the characters are well drawn, whether they are based on original observation and whether they give us the feeling that we are in contact with a living person. Notice whether the author has shown how the character has changed in the course of the novel or whether no change is observable; this may make the difference between a major and a minor character. Another matter that needs attention is the background, which may consist of description of the society in which the characters move, or of the place, or even of the traditions and ideas which influence them. In the case of *Nostromo* we can see that Conrad attempts to satisfy our interest in all these respects.

The most vital part of an analysis, however, is only reached when we begin to consider the deeper questions of form. This means that we think of the work as the product of a certain period and as the result of certain tendencies in the history of literature. We are now concerned with the method and the purpose of the author, and if we can decide what these may have been, it is possible to judge whether the writer has been successful. It is obviously a mistake to blame Conrad, for instance, for not showing us the childhood of Nostromo if his purpose was not to describe his life but rather to show him in the more significant moments of his later development. We must to a certain extent judge a work through the eyes of the artist himself.

Finally, our analysis should be completed by a general assessment based on everything we have discovered so far and in addition by an attempt to see the work as a whole, regardless of individual details. This is not always easy, for our judgement may easily be deformed by our own prejudices or lack of knowledge. In any work of art we make contact with the character of the artist himself and this may make it hard for us to be objective, just as we may be unable to like or understand a person we meet if for some reason their appearance annoys us. Thus we must try to separate our personal reaction from our impersonal judgment. To give an example, one reader may be greatly attracted by any novel that describes distant countries; such a reader will share Conrad's own interest and will be inclined to praise *Nostromo* as a book. A different reader might be quite uninterested in travel and thus see much less value in the work. Both these judgments might be said to be based on personal prejudice and therefore to be not really satisfactory.

Suggestions about how to answer questions

If you intend to take an examination in which a book such as *Nostromo* is a subject for study, the following suggestions may be found helpful.

1. Read the book carefully and do not be satisfied with one quick reading. You will need to re-read certain important passages several times.
2. Go through the suggested questions on the text and write out answers to them. Do not be content with just thinking what you might say. It will greatly help you if you take the trouble to do written answers; they may be in the form of notes, if preferred, but you should put them on paper. You will then be far more ready to answer any question put to you in the exam.
3. Practise writing answers in the time allotted in the exam. Answering examination questions is a strictly practical matter and it has often been noticed that good examination results can be obtained by candidates who are apparently less capable than others who fail the exam. This is usually because they stick to the point and do not waste time. The examination room is not the place to think, but the place to *write*! A good candidate has already thought sufficiently about his subject before he starts the exam; his written answers come naturally and quickly.
4. It is a matter of choice whether the candidate writes out notes on a separate sheet of paper before starting an answer. A few brief notes as reminders of what the candidate has to say are probably best. The essential thing is not to waste time.
5. It is obvious that clear handwriting is one of the first passports to success. Handwriting that is easy to read shows politeness towards the reader, in this case the examiner—and it is always appreciated.

Bad handwriting confuses the examiner, makes his job harder and puts him in a bad mood. Words that have been corrected should be re-written entirely, so that the spelling is completely clear and the whole word easily legible. If letters are left that might be read in more than one way, the examiner has a right to conclude that the student is not sure of the spelling, and will take marks off as a result. Usually, in a literature paper, the examiner is more interested in what the student has to say than in how he says it, but a certain standard of correctness must be maintained all the same.

6. Just as clear handwriting is a help for the examiner, so also is clear exposition of the candidate's ideas. It is normally considered that each answer should follow the rules of any good composition, which means that the opening sentence should show that the candidate has understood the question. The main body of the answer should continue the same line of thought, without too many extra ideas being introduced. Finally, the answer should conclude with a sentence or short paragraph that links up all that has been said, so that the examiner will feel that there has been some sort of plan behind the answer and that it has not all been written in a confused way from the first ideas that have come to the candidate's mind. A good conclusion helps to make sense of everything that has gone before.
7. Be careful to use a sufficient number of paragraphs. There is no definite rule about when to open a new paragraph; obviously, too many paragraphs are disturbing and give the impression that the writer is trying to show how many different points he has to make. On the other hand, paragraphs that are too long make one feel that the writer has got involved in his thoughts and consequently the reader—in this case, the examiner—hesitates at the effort before reading. A long paragraph always has something uninviting about it. But hard-and-fast rules cannot be given; the important thing is that any major change of subject or a new point in any argument always requires a new paragraph, and this must not be forgotten.
8. When choosing words or phrases to express your thought, always prefer the simplest and most direct. If necessary, divide up your idea and express it through more than one phrase. Do not try to impress the reader by clever phrases of which you yourself hardly know the meaning. Write down what you think and avoid using terms that you have found in books just because they seem striking. Nothing is more quickly noticed by an examiner than an attempt to use an 'impressive' vocabulary; it is a very usual mistake of candidates, particularly bad candidates, and it should at all costs be avoided.

9. When writing answers on literature, avoid writing in a vague or abstract way. The candidate should make clear to the examiner that he knows what he is talking about and show that his ideas are related to a real knowledge of the texts and not just remembered from the comments of critics. Therefore you should always try to give as many examples as necessary to explain each point that is made. These examples should be taken from the text that has to be studied, or other books by the same author. They may be examples of incidents, types of character, ways of speaking or even the words used (but it will not be found practicable to try to remember long quotations). Notice that the model answers on Conrad support every statement by concrete proof. Remember that this sort of writing is what is naturally preferred by the English mind; remember—not abstract, but concrete.
10. To sum up what has been said: the main things are to know your subject well, especially the texts to be studied; to practise writing answers in the time provided; to write clearly and simply.

Examples of possible questions

Here are some questions you could study after reading *Nostromo*, following the method of analysis already described. If we take first the external sides, such as Conrad's evocation of people and places and the action, we might begin by thinking about the following points:

(*a*) which characters seem to you to be best drawn and why?

(*b*) how far are the individual characters essential to the main action of the story? Are there characters which could be left out without seriously altering the book?

(*c*) do you consider that Conrad has succeeded in showing the different characters as typical of their nationalities, English, Italian or Spanish?

(*d*) which incidents in the course of the story do you find best described? Are the most dramatic moments always the best or do you find significance also in quieter parts of the story?

(*e*) what are the characteristics of the people living in Sulaco and Costaguana? In what points of the story do these characteristics become clear and how far do they affect the course of the story?

(*f*) make a list of the virtues and the defects of the different characters. How far do these virtues and defects influence the course of the story and the part that each character plays in the story?

(*g*) what does Conrad say about the country itself and of its history and geography? How far do these points directly affect the story? Do you consider that the author could have cut short any of his descriptions or are they essential to give the full message of the book?

When we have carefully considered the above questions and found our answers, we are then in a position to turn to the more difficult matters of form and method. It may help if we think of the external side already discussed as What? and the questions of form as representing How? and Why? Naturally the author himself did not separate these things in his mind in this artificial way, but it is useful for us to do so as it enables us to feel sure that we have not missed some significant point. We might begin by asking ourselves the following questions:

(*h*) how far does *Nostromo* resemble other novels of the same period, and others written earlier or later?

(*i*) how far does Conrad go beyond the question of Nostromo's own life and to what extent is the inclusion of this other material justified?

(*j*) how is the story presented to the reader? What do you think are the reasons for Conrad's choice of his method of presentation? (In other words, why does Conrad not describe everything that happens in chronological sequence, that is, in the same order that the events occur?)

(*k*) what do you think are Conrad's main interests as revealed in the book? What characters does he especially praise or condemn, and why?

(*l*) make a list of what are in your opinion the good and bad points of the novel, and in each case consider if a different reader might possibly have a very different opinion, and why.

How to study 'books about books'

One of the most difficult problems that confront any student of literature, especially if he is taking examinations, is how to form a satisfactory picture of the books within the setting in which they were written. The student needs to know something about the author, something about other authors of the same period and something about the general cultural tradition which helped to form the books.

These Notes should be regarded as an introduction. Other books should be consulted. Different ways of looking at Conrad should be studied; we have indicated some of them, thinking of him as a foreign observer, as a man of action, as a writer with certain traditions behind him, as an author aiming at success. He can be thought of as a product of a social environment, with his upbringing and his experience of revolution, or even as a product of economic conditions, so that his books can be seen as the expression of a middle or upper-class world. He can also be thought of as a writer who showed the way to others who later copied some of his tricks of style.

To get some idea of these different points of view, it may be wise to study several books, reading them quite quickly, rather than concentrate too much on one book on the subject, however good. The student should get hold of the following types of book:

(1) general histories of literature,
(2) biographical studies,
(3) studies on the general culture of the period,
(4) simple history books, especially on social history.

Before going into details about Conrad, it may be helpful to comment on these different types:

1. General histories of literature should be chosen, at first at least, for their simple and broad treatment. They should be short for preference. The student should possess at least two such books to which he can refer quickly in connection with any author, or period he may be reading about. It does not matter that these books repeat more or less the same ideas about any given author; what the student has to do is to get hold of these facts, and it will help to read about them in two or more slightly different texts.
2. Biographical studies are useful in order to get a feeling of the author as a human being, but too much time must not be spent on them, for the life of a writer has often very little to do with his work, which is what the student is concerned with. Biographies, however, often contain chapters devoted to certain books or certain aspects of the author's writing and these may be valuable.
3. Studies of the general culture of the period need to be chosen carefully for, like biographies, they may lead the student into too much detail. Illustrated books of a 'popular' or even elementary kind should not be despised. The student needs to understand something of the 'background'. This helps to explain why the author was interested in certain subjects and why he treated them as he did. It is unwise to pay too much attention to studies that are detailed or one-sided.
4. History books should be selected which do not go into political details, but which concentrate rather on broad social tendencies; in other words, books on 'social history' are what are needed—often such histories are very closely connected with the themes of an author and may even quote from his books to explain their points.

Hints about studying texts

If you are studying a text such as *Nostromo* for an examination, the following suggestions may help you:

1. A thorough knowledge of the text is the first requirement. The summaries provided in these notes are intended to help you to understand the full story and to remind you of any details you may not notice.
2. Make written notes about the characters. If you start with the points mentioned in this booklet, you should try to find examples of both speech and action. For instance, Nostromo's vanity is mentioned and we recall the present of silver buttons to show how he liked to be dramatically generous; look for other examples of this tendency. Take each character and decide what passages in the book reveal their nature best.
3. Make a list of the themes that can be seen in *Nostromo*, beginning with the main ideas mentioned in this booklet such as 'material interests', heroism, fear, violence, etc. Again find concrete examples apart from those we have quoted. Try to connect these examples with other stories by Conrad, which you should read if possible—the suggestions for further reading will help you to choose.
4. Do not just concentrate on *Nostromo*. Once you have got a grasp of the plot and the significance of the characters, aim to understand Conrad as an author and man. To do this, you will have to read other books about him and his place in English literature.

Model answers

The three model answers which follow are intended to show the way in which an examination question should be treated, and at the same time to mention various subjects which have not been discussed earlier.

Students, especially foreign students, may feel that they could not express themselves like this. But remember the main thing is the method. When you write, do not worry about how much you know; instead concentrate on the problems of introducing the subject well, developing it and concluding. The other essential thing is to give concrete examples to prove your points—never be vague, always be precise!

Our three answers are arranged in order of difficulty for different levels of study.

Conrad seems to have different attitudes towards the characters in the novel—can you define what these attitudes are and explain their connection with Conrad's own philosophy of life? Give references to the text to back up all your ideas

We often feel that Conrad is a man of strong prejudices as we read his books, and *Nostromo* is no exception. It even seems that he loses interest when he is dealing with certain types of character and as a result the story at some points suddenly seems boring or at least lacking in its usual sparkle. Perhaps the arrival in Sulaco of Martin Decoud might be given as an example of such a moment when we have the impression that Conrad's attitude is rather negative towards this supercilious young man.

To take the main character first—Nostromo; he is clearly in many ways a hero after Conrad's own heart and although he makes many mistakes and has many defects we sense that Conrad is willing to be kind in his interpretation. His vanity, for instance, comes out clearly at various points, when we see him riding through the crowds on the day of the President's visit and when he accepts tasks that may be unrewarding or difficult but which he could not refuse without spoiling his reputation; an example of this is the greatest job of all, the secret removal of the silver by boat at night. Then we also are allowed to see that Nostromo is not inspired by any true ideal of service, but that he works well only as long as he feels that he will be respected or admired for what he does. So when the head of the railway company came to inspect the construction work they were carrying out, Nostromo was proud to be given the responsibility of looking after him and organised his journey for him across difficult country in a way that nobody else could have managed. If he was given a job that offered a real challenge to his physical strength and endurance or, equally important, to his powers of leadership (as head of the lightermen), then Nostromo could be depended on and Conrad gives him full credit for this. He was a true man and had the stuff that heroes are made of. He is not capable of deep thought—all his actions are carried out instinctively—and Conrad shows his confusion of mind when, about the time of the removal of the treasure, he begins to feel that he is being exploited by his employers. But he always remains equal to any situation, for he has courage and dignity, right up to his very death. While smiling at his weaknesses, Conrad admires him.

A complete contrast is offered by Señor Hirsch, whom Conrad describes with evident irony and contempt. His greatest fault is cowardice; also in direct contrast to Nostromo is his attitude to money. Hirsch is a small-minded trader, alert to opportunities for buying and selling, probably basically honest. He comes to Sulaco because he sees that money could be made there and he makes persevering efforts to get Charles Gould on his side. Nostromo, on the other hand, is a great adventurer who again and again is shown working for reasons other than money; when finally he succumbs to the temptation of the silver, it is not any petty act of dishonesty but a magnificent danger that he faces with the possibility of riches that will set him high above other men.

Conrad also shows irony in his description of Captain Mitchell and the way he talks. But it is not a contemptuous irony—we feel almost that there are two points in his favour that Conrad never forgets—he was a sailor and he was English! So Conrad draws a picture of a rather pompous old fellow who is not very sensitive to the finer points of life. He appreciates Nostromo's qualities but he does not notice his growing dissatisfaction. When he is arrested by Sotillo's soldiers, he is angry and loses control, but he is never afraid. He is a somewhat boring companion, as when he takes his guests round Sulaco, but he is kind, loyal and dependable.

Charles Gould is another character for whom Conrad shows a certain forgiveness. Like Nostromo, he is a man on a large scale with the quality of energy that Conrad always seems to admire. He goes under—that is to say, he loses his way in life, in Conrad's opinion—not so much because of his fanaticism, as because he comes under the strange spell of the silver that later exercises its power over Nostromo also. Conrad is full of sympathy for Charles in his early days and paints an attractive picture of his idealistic enthusiasm at the time of his marriage, when he finds support in his wife's true love.

Another character who is described with a certain respectful pity is Don José Avellanos. His enthusiasm and idealism attract Conrad, but his idealism is misplaced; perhaps Conrad feels above all that he suffered from the ignorance of all politicians, for even the best must believe in the value of their own action and this is something that Conrad in his pessimism often seems to deny. He seems to think that politics, after all, lead nowhere. Life does not go forward in the direct line of progress; things certainly change, but not always really for the better. So the description of Sulaco in its later prosperity is a direct reflection on Don José's statesmanship. He helped to guide his country out of brutal and primitive conditions, but corruption and cruelty are part of human nature and do not disappear.

So through his characters, as well as through his plot, Conrad shows his own very individual and clearly marked personality. We feel his presence in the background as the author who was also a man of action, someone who was a clear-sighted judge of other men, but who had also understanding and compassion for their inevitable weaknesses.

The structure of Conrad's novels is invariably strengthened by ideas or themes that lie in the background and give meaning to the plot. Discuss with reference to *Nostromo*

When we read Conrad we constantly get the impression that we are listening to a man telling a story that has some special significance for him and which illustrates some point about life that he has learnt through experience. This impression is naturally particularly strong in stories which are told in the first person such as *Heart of Darkness* or where there is a narrator introduced at the beginning, as in *Youth*, told by the often recurring figure of the old sailor Marlow. It may be that the point to be illustrated about life is in fact its pointlessness—and some of Conrad's stories come very close to concentrating on just that—or it may be some strange paradox in human nature or some remarkable adventure, but we always seem to notice that what Conrad has to recount, fits into his own special scheme of things; he has thought it all out and it means something.

In *Nostromo* the very title indicates that the novel centres round one man and it would be right to look first at him to find what lessons or thoughts Conrad aims to pass on to us. What seems clear from the start is that this is a hero who, in spite of his obvious strength and typically 'heroic' qualities, suffers from serious limitations. By choosing a man who is uneducated and who owes his success to his character, not to any intellectual gifts, Conrad is able to stress the emptiness of a man before he is taken possession of by an idea—in Nostromo's case, by the idea of saving the treasure for himself. It is not so much the crime that Conrad brings out—for he makes it clear that what Nostromo is trying to keep, represents only a tiny part of the almost infinite riches of the mine or of what Gould and his Concession are able to continue to extract. What Conrad is interested in is the way in which a man is corrupted inwardly and he shows the ease with which Nostromo sells himself to the Devil, as old-fashioned religion would have expressed it. Indeed, once the opportunity has occurred, there is no point at which Nostromo seems to make any resistance to the temptation to pretend that the treasure has been sunk. It is partly because Dr Monygham jumps to conclusions and partly because Nostromo has begun to be oppressed by the feeling that he is being exploited by the rich white leaders in Sulaco.

This process of inner corruption is what gives point to the story of Nostromo and it gains extra force by the parallel examples that Conrad also provides, the most striking of which is Charles Gould himself. Here we have a man who does not have the excuse, as it were, that he is untaught or uneducated and cannot foresee the moral dangers that will surround him. Furthermore, he is not alone, but has his wife who, if he had allowed her to do so, would have communicated to him a saner view of life and a sense of proportion that would have prevented him from doing what he did—which was also really the same as Nostromo, selling his soul to the devil of one idea. The subtle complication in his case lies in the fact that he was originally inspired by the fine ideal of carrying out the task that his father had abandoned, an ideal which at the beginning had gained the full weight of his wife's support. Thus good leads to bad, Conrad seems to say in further comment, and in both men the extent of their moral downfall is only increased by their qualities of energy and will.

A less attractive example of possession—at least this is clearly Conrad's view—is provided by the fanaticism of the priest, Corbelán. Conrad shares, it seems, the anti-clerical opinions of old Viola, the Garibaldian, and of Nostromo himself, and he does not paint an agreeable picture of the misplaced heroism that had inspired this priest to wander alone for years in the forest in the service of his missionary task. Conrad seems to be offering us here a figure that stands close to the perilously narrow borderland that separates fanaticism from madness. This was the borderland that the strange Kurtz in *Heart of Darkness* crossed, and Conrad perhaps was putting his finger on a central problem of the modern world where power and violence can so easily get out of control.

We cannot help noticing the contrast furnished on the other hand by two more old-fashioned types whose portraits also are sketched with considerable detail—Don José Avellanos and Captain Mitchell. These two cannot be compared with each other but they show varying forms of mixed success and failure in life. In Don José Conrad is portraying a liberal idealism that stands in contrast to the religious absolutism of his brother-in-law the priest. The guiding idea here is that moderate and humane views are always in danger of being overthrown by extremism and brutal violence—symbolised by the Montero brothers. Nobody who has studied history can say that Conrad is wrong. Yet Don José is not entirely a failure, for he has helped to guide his country through a phase of its political education.

As regards Captain Mitchell, it may be said that his happy ignorance of his own mediocrity is connected with another theme that haunts all the work of Conrad and the story of Nostromo as much as any other—and this theme is the irony of Fate. Conrad is intensely conscious of the fact that so often things turn out the opposite of what was expected and, as has already been said, good becomes bad. Sometimes even bad turns into good, but Conrad stresses this rather less! However, Captain Mitchell, at the end of the book, is in a position to observe the way in which the struggles and disasters of an earlier period have led to a calm conclusion, with prosperity for the people and a reasonable political settlement, which could not have been easily foreseen. Decoud and Nostromo, who have played vital, though very different, parts, both disappear and leave the stage to others who reap the benefit, while those who remain, such as Mitchell and Gould, seem to have lost any power to change or develop—there is little hope for the soul of Charles Gould.

So Conrad may truly be said to have written a novel which has a lining of deeply considered thought underneath the elaborate surface detail of incident and character. Reading such a book, apart from the interest of the story, we have contact with the mind of a writer who, in spite of obvious bias towards pessimism and despair, has observed much, lived a full life and given us the fruit of true experience.

‘Conrad—a poet among novelists.’ Discuss

Whatever ‘poetry’ means, it seems at least to be something *different*. In this sense, the word appears to be a most appropriate description for Joseph Conrad as a novelist. This quality of being different is often ascribed, rather too glibly, to the fact that he was a foreigner, implying that everything can be explained if we remember that, although he wrote in English, he contributed an essentially Polish point of view of life and something Continental in his approach to the technical problems of novel-writing. This is true, but it is not the whole truth. For Conrad’s work is permeated through and through with a vivid and personal sense of reality that can only be described as poetic and which has nothing to do with technique or rationality.

It is significant that his most ambitious novel should centre round the life of a man whom Fate separated from other men, first by his easy assumption of natural pre-eminence and later by the poisonous influence of a secret. Indeed it does not take long to draw up a list of other stories in which the basic theme is that of a man apart who sees life as an adventure with perpetual surprises. Almayer, Lord Jim, Kurtz in *Heart of Darkness*, Nostromo, Prince Roman, are all unusual people in one way or another, condemned to solitude in the midst of their fellow-men, dissatisfied yet energetic, and doomed to wander through the world or through life without ever being able to settle down comfortably or be reconciled to the ordinary. The sea itself, that shares with human characters the chief rôle in so many of Conrad’s novels, is invariably associated with adventure and change and yearning. It is obvious that the sea was the very mirror of Conrad’s soul and it is never wholly absent from his stories, even when the setting is on shore or inland—thus Nostromo’s life centres round ships and it is on an island that he hides his treasure and eventually meets his death.

The objection that Conrad never wrote in verse hardly needs discussing. A versifier is very clearly not the same as a poet and we have too often heard great literature described as poetic to be surprised if Conrad's prose is said to contain a strong element of poetry. It is not so much the form that counts, as the spirit behind it. Much of the Bible is great poetry, even when rendered in some prose translation which may have little elegance, though, obviously, when beauty of language is allied to the inspiration of the idea, the name of poetry is even more justified. Conrad's work has both of these qualities. Even though he handled the English language with a certain artificial care—or perhaps precisely because he does do so—we are always conscious of this special gift for finding just the right word, for summing up a whole mood in a single phrase. What better example of this could be found than the end of Nostromo with the image of the silver cloud?—'a big white cloud shining like a mass of solid silver, the genius of the magnificent Capataz de Cargadores dominated the dark gulf containing his conquests of treasure and love.' This is fine writing that deserves to be called both beautiful and poetic—even if there is a slight touch of self-consciousness, perhaps a hint of melodrama.

This little weakness of Conrad's that sometimes leads him, identifying with his hero, to take up postures of almost Byronic gloom, may make the reader doubt the validity of his philosophy of life. We may feel the presence of this pessimism too strongly to be able to accept his conclusions derived from such an emotional source; like Hardy, he is tempted to overload the plot with twists that are intended to prove the malevolence of Fate. But the reason is that he has too powerful a sense of individuality and of the strangeness of life and to get this essentially Romantic message across, he feels obliged to underline it with the aid of an image or some potent symbol. The crucified body of Hirsch signals a message of horror to the reader, as well as to the Doctor and Nostromo who discover it.

But perhaps the most convincing reason for thinking of Conrad as a poet is his omnipresent sense of beauty. His nightmare scenes of torture and often prolonged descriptions of failure are negative, but they are the reverse of the coin that, on the other side, reveals significance in the smallest gestures and the most neglected corners of a man's personality. Dr Monygham's slow climb to restored self-respect is beautifully and delicately shown; in addition we learn that he never acquires the ability to conceal his overflowing sensitivity except under a sardonic mask that can give pleasure to no one. Good and bad are inextricably mingled and Conrad the observer can see poetic meaning in both. With this gift, it is not surprising that he allowed himself to accompany every incident and description of character with some personal comment or philosophical interpretation. This running commentary is strictly a luxury from the point of view of the story-teller, whose job it is to interest and entertain us with a story. But Conrad is concerned with something more than prosaic facts; he does not question their importance or the validity of the material world with all its tragedies, but he always shows his awareness of something behind—the world of poetic significance which contains the true action of his novels, for it is here that people like Charles Gould and his wife, Dr Monygham and Nostromo live out their lives with their inner failure or success which often runs ironically counter to their visible careers.

Part 5

Suggestions for further reading

The text

These Notes refer to pages in the Everyman Edition, Dent, London, 1957, reprinted 1966. There is a Penguin Books edition, Harmondsworth, 1963. See *A note on the text*, p.10.

Other works by Conrad

Almayer's Folly, 1895
The Nigger of the Narcissus, 1898
Lord Jim, 1900
Heart of Darkness, 1902
Youth, 1902
Typhoon, 1903
The Secret Agent, 1907
Under Western Eyes, 1911
The Shadow Line, 1917
Tales of Hearsay, 1925

The above stories will be found published by Dent or Penguin. *Heart of Darkness* and *Youth* are particularly recommended; also *Tales of Hearsay* (long short stories).

General histories of English literature

Every student should be familiar with the general tendencies in English literature, recent and otherwise.

THORNLEY, G.C.: *Outline of English Literature*, Longman Background Series, London, 1968. An illustrated paperback.

BURGESS, ANTONY: *English Literature*, Longman, London, 1974. Illustrated.

THOMPSON, DENYS: *What to read in English Literature*, Heinemann, London, 1975.

EVANS, IFOR: *Short History of English Literature*, Pelican, London, 1940; 2nd edition 1963. This book does not present authors biographically but is useful to read together with one of the previous three.

More detailed histories of English literature

FRASER, G.S.: *The Modern Writer and his World*, A. Deutsch, London, 1964. This deals with the period from 1890s to today. Only a few pages on Conrad, but clearly written and a good general introduction.

SAMPSON, G.: *Concise Cambridge History of English Literature* (chapter on Age of T.S. Eliot by R.C. Churchill) Cambridge University Press, Cambridge, 1961. This is useful as general summary and reminder of facts.

LEGOUIS, E.: *Short History of English Literature*, Oxford University Press, Oxford, 1934. Also contains the main general facts.

FORD, BORIS ed.: *Guide to English Literature, the Modern Age*, Penguin Books, Harmondsworth, 1961 (last volume of *Penguin Guide to English Literature*).

ROBSON, W.W.: *Modern English Literature*, Oxford University Press, London, 1970. This book, as well as the following two, is probably more suitable for the already advanced student.

DAICHES, D.: *Critical History of English Literature*, Vol 2, Secker & Warburg, London, 1961. Only one page on Conrad, but advanced discussion of his contemporaries.

BERGONZI, B. ed.: *History of Literature in the English Language*, Vol 7, 'The Twentieth Century', Barrie & Jenkins, London, 1970. See chapter 1, 'Advent of Modernism'.

Studies of Conrad

BAINES, JOCELYN: *Joseph Conrad—A critical biography*, Weidenfeld & Nicolson, London, 1960. This concentrates on Conrad's life, but also contains good chapters on books, including 'Nostromo'.

COX, C.B.: *J. Conrad—the Modern Imagination*, Dent, London, 1974. Non-biographical, this concentrates on certain main books and themes. Discusses technique, psychological interpretations, with reference also to other studies on Conrad. This book, like the two following, is probably suitable for the more advanced student.

HEWITT, D.: *Conrad—A Reassessment*, Bowes & Bowes, London, 1952; 2nd edition 1969. A detailed study, using advanced critical vocabulary, this concentrates on main books.

GUERARD, A.J.: *Conrad the Novelist*, Harvard University Press, Cambridge, Mass., USA, 1966. This also goes into detailed questions of literary technique.

SHERRY, NORMAN: *Conrad and his World*, Thames & Hudson, London, 1972. Largely biographical, with 142 illustrations.

General studies on the English novel

DAICHES, DAVID: *The Novel and the Modern World*, Phoenix, Chicago & London, 1965. This contains chapters on D.H. Lawrence and James Joyce, as well as on Conrad (40 pages). A useful, general discussion.

ALLEN, WALTER: *The English Novel*, Phoenix House, London, 1954. Some ten pages on Conrad; a technical approach.

LEAVIS, F.R.: *The Great Tradition*, Peregrine Books, London, 1962. A difficult book, but much studied and quoted, which contains some 50 pages on Conrad, with especial praise for *Nostromo*.

BOULTON, MARJORIE: *Anatomy of the Novel*, Routledge, London, 1975. A discussion of points of technique such as verisimilitude, character and conversation.

CECIL, DAVID: *Poets and Story-Tellers*, Constable, London. Well-written, with chapters on two contemporaries of Conrad—Virginia Woolf and E.M. Forster.

General historical background

TREVELYAN, G.M.: *English Social History*, Longman, London, 1942. The best known general social history, and perhaps still the best. Available in illustrated editions.

ROBSON, W.: *Twentieth Century Britain*, Oxford University Press, London, 1973. A fair amount of political history; illustrated.

PRIESTLEY, J.B.: *The Edwardians*, Heinemann, London, 1970. A book for non-experts; lively, interesting and well-illustrated.

HIBBERT, C.: *Social History of Victorian Britain*, Angus & Robertson, London, 1975. Interesting illustrations.

The author of these notes

Anthony Strange, with a Cambridge degree in Modern Languages and History, has long experience of teaching foreign students. Beginning in Italy and France, where he taught in Paris for seven years, he now works in London. His teaching has always been equally divided between language and literature.

YORK NOTES

The first 100 titles

CHINUA ACHEBE	*Arrow of God* *Things Fall Apart*
JANE AUSTEN	*Northanger Abbey* *Pride and Prejudice* *Sense and Sensibility*
ROBERT BOLT	*A Man For All Seasons*
CHARLOTTE BRONTË	*Jane Eyre*
EMILY BRONTË	*Wuthering Heights*
ALBERT CAMUS	*L'Etranger (The Outsider)*
GEOFFREY CHAUCER	*Prologue to the Canterbury Tales* *The Franklin's Tale* *The Knight's Tale* *The Nun's Priest's Tale* *The Pardoner's Tale*
SIR ARTHUR CONAN DOYLE	*The Hound of the Baskervilles*
JOSEPH CONRAD	*Nostromo*
DANIEL DEFOE	*Robinson Crusoe*
CHARLES DICKENS	*David Copperfield* *Great Expectations*
GEORGE ELIOT	*Adam Bede* *Silas Marner* *The Mill on the Floss*
T.S. ELIOT	*The Waste Land*
WILLIAM FAULKNER	*As I Lay Dying*
F. SCOTT FITZGERALD	*The Great Gatsby*
E.M. FORSTER	*A Passage to India*
ATHOL FUGARD	*Selected Plays*
MRS GASKELL	*North and South*

WILLIAM GOLDING	*Lord of the Flies*
OLIVER GOLDSMITH	*The Vicar of Wakefield*
THOMAS HARDY	*Jude the Obscure* *Tess of the D'Urbervilles* *The Mayor of Casterbridge* *The Return of the Native* *The Trumpet Major*
L.P. HARTLEY	*The Go-Between*
ERNEST HEMINGWAY	*For Whom the Bell Tolls* *The Old Man and the Sea*
ANTHONY HOPE	*The Prisoner of Zenda*
RICHARD HUGHES	*A High Wind in Jamaica*
THOMAS HUGHES	*Tom Brown's Schooldays*
HENRIK IBSEN	*A Doll's House*
HENRY JAMES	*The Turn of the Screw*
BEN JONSON	*The Alchemist* *Volpone*
D.H. LAWRENCE	*Sons and Lovers* *The Rainbow*
HARPER LEE	*To Kill a Mocking-Bird*
SOMERSET MAUGHAM	*Selected Short Stories*
HERMAN MELVILLE	*Billy Budd* *Moby Dick*
ARTHUR MILLER	*Death of a Salesman* *The Crucible*
JOHN MILTON	*Paradise Lost I & II*
SEAN O'CASEY	*Juno and the Paycock*
GEORGE ORWELL	*Animal Farm* *Nineteen Eighty-four*
JOHN OSBORNE	*Look Back in Anger*
HAROLD PINTER	*The Birthday Party*
J.D. SALINGER	*The Catcher in the Rye*
SIR WALTER SCOTT	*Ivanhoe* *Quentin Durward*

WILLIAM SHAKESPEARE	*A Midsummer Night's Dream* *Antony and Cleopatra* *Coriolanus* *Cymbeline* *Hamlet* *Henry IV Part I* *Henry V* *Julius Caesar* *King Lear* *Macbeth* *Measure for Measure* *Othello* *Richard II* *Romeo and Juliet* *The Merchant of Venice* *The Tempest* *The Winter's Tale* *Troilus and Cressida* *Twelfth Night*
GEORGE BERNARD SHAW	*Androcles and the Lion* *Arms and the Man* *Caesar and Cleopatra* *Pygmalion*
RICHARD BRINSLEY SHERIDAN	*The School for Scandal*
JOHN STEINBECK	*Of Mice and Men* *The Grapes of Wrath* *The Pearl*
ROBERT LOUIS STEVENSON	*Kidnapped* *Treasure Island*
JONATHAN SWIFT	*Gulliver's Travels*
W.M. THACKERAY	*Vanity Fair*
MARK TWAIN	*Huckleberry Finn* *Tom Sawyer*
VOLTAIRE	*Candide*
H.G. WELLS	*The History of Mr Polly* *The Invisible Man* *The War of the Worlds*
OSCAR WILDE	*The Importance of Being Earnest*